Words Fail Me

WHAT
EVERYONE
WHO
WRITES

Words Fail Me

SHOULD
KNOW
ABOUT
WRITING

Patricia T. O'Conner

Harcourt Brace & Company
New York   San Diego   London

Requests for permission to make copies of any part of the work
should be mailed to: Permissions Department, Harcourt, Inc.,
6277 Sea Harbor Drive, Orlando, Florida 32887-6777.

Library of Congress Cataloging-in-Publication Data
O'Conner, Patricia T.
Words fail me: what everyone who writes should know
about writing/by Patricia T. O'Conner
p.   cm.
Includes index.
ISBN 0-15-100371-8
1. Authorship.   2. Creative writing.   3. Report writing.
I. Title.
PN147.027   1999
808'.02—dc21   99-25610

Designed by Lydia D'moch
Printed in the United States of America
First edition
E D C B

For my mother

Contents

Acknowledgments

It occurs to me that this book has no advice about how to write acknowledgments. Hey, what better place to remedy the oversight?

Authors write acknowledgments to acknowledge their debts, of course, to thank the people who helped in some way. Ideally, your tone should be gracious but not queenly, grateful but not groveling. Humble dignity is what you should aim for. Acknowledgments also enable you to shamelessly drop names without seeming immodest. In this way, you let the reader know that while you, the author, did the real work, a great many important people stopped whatever they were doing to give you a hand. (You may not be bosom buddies with them all, but who's to know?)

The impressive bunch that helped with this book includes Laurie Asséo, Ann Beattie, Alida Becker, André Bernard, D. J. R. Bruckner, Jo Ellyn Clarey, Charles Doherty, Hugh Downs, David Feldman, Margalit Fox, Rob Franciosi, Samuel G. Freedman, Elizabeth Frenchman, Ken Gordon, Robert R. Harris, Jennifer Hartig, Dimitra Karras, Panayota Karras, Allen Kellerman, Craig Kellerman, David Kelly, Mitchel Levitas, Eden Ross Lipson, Rose McAllister, Charles McGrath, Kate Murphy, Deborah Nye, Lamont Olson, Jeanne Pinder, David Rampe, Tad Richards, Tim Sacco, Robert Schulmann, Michael Sniffen, Yves Tourre, Gloria Gardiner Urban, Bruce Washburn, Elizabeth Weis, and Marilynn K. Yee. I'm also grateful to my sister, Kathy Richard, and to Larry and Pamela Kellerman for their support and encouragement.

I owe special thanks to my extraordinary editor, Jane Isay, who asked me to write this book and whose uncanny vision kept it on track. Dan Green, my agent, knows much more about writing than I, and his advice was invaluable. Herbert Mitgang, Marilyn Stasio, and Peter Keepnews were tireless and inexhaustible sources whose literary sleuthing made my job easier. John Allen Paulos, God's gift to the numerically insecure, offered advice on the chapter about mathematics. And once again, Anna Jardine proved that a good copy editor is a pearl beyond price.

My husband, Stewart Kellerman, was virtually a co-author. He got me out of more jams than I can count, and his wisdom shows on every page. Finally, I owe a bottomless debt to Beverly J. Newman, who was never too busy to take two little girls to the library. Thanks, Mom.

Two days into my first newspaper job and itching to see my name in print, I picked up a ringing phone and took the call that I thought would launch a glittering career.

The man on the other end said he had a dog so intelligent that it took its meals seated at the table with the rest of the family. Not only did this dog have its own chair and its own place setting, but it refrained from eating until grace was said, then waited to be excused from the table. Would I be interested in doing a story?

Would I! I rushed up to the hard-boiled city editor, visions of a page-one byline dancing in my head. "Mr.

Murphy," I said, "I have somebody on the phone with a great human-interest story."

"It's *Murphy*!" he said, spitting cigar smoke. (In those days, ashtrays were standard office equipment.) "What've you got?"

I told him my great story.

Silence.

"It even wears a bib," I added.

Murphy rolled his cigar to the other side of his mouth. "No dog stories," he said. "I hate dog stories. If we run a story today about a dog that dines at the table, we'll have to run one tomorrow about a dog that dances *Swan Lake*."

"But what do I tell the guy on the phone?"

"That's your problem. Now get me some news!"

It was my first on-the-job lesson. The lesson wasn't "No dog stories," though. It was "Write for Murphy."

Many years and many jobs and many bosses later, I still try to write for Murphy. Not the real Murphy, long buried now, but whoever is going to read what I write. And no matter how many people I'm writing for, I try to talk to one reader at a time.

I owe many of the tips in this book to the editors and writers I've worked with since that first job at the *Waterloo Courier* in Iowa more than twenty-five years ago. Some of these folks have been hard to ignore. One of my bosses liked to blow up paper bags and pop them just to make sure everybody was awake. Another was able to balance a spoon on the end of his nose while reciting the first few lines of Milton's *Paradise Lost*. Another had to be roused from bed every morning by a copyboy whose job it was to make sure the boss got to work. Nothing about these people was prosaic, least of all their prose. They were the ones in the balcony; if I could please them, the rest of the audience would take care of itself.

Contrary to popular opinion, there's no mystery to writing well. It's a skill that just about anyone can learn, more craft than art. When words fail us, as they often do, the reasons are usually simple. So are the solutions. They can be as easy as breaking a sentence in two or moving a word somewhere else. The term "writing" covers a lot of ground. But whether your work ends up in a history professor's e-mail, a marketing report, a community newsletter, or a best-selling novel, the pitfalls are the same. *Words Fail Me* is about techniques for making poor writing presentable and good writing even better. Think of it as a user's manual for words.

And words, written words, are getting a workout these days, in case you haven't noticed. Suddenly we're a nation of writers. By putting a keyboard in every lap, it seems, the computer has changed the way we communicate, virtually overnight. If we think of writing as conversation, everybody seems to be talking at once.

Who *isn't* wired? Teenagers no longer spend their evenings yakking on the phone. They send gossipy e-mail or instant messages, hang out in chat rooms, and write. Executives who once dictated letters now click on Reply and write. College students can trade notes in newsgroups, question their professors, and turn in assignments without leaving their dorms. Gardeners, golfers, military brats, parents for and against spanking, aspiring actors, quilters, gym teachers, plastic surgeons, dog trainers, arthritis sufferers, geologists, and pizza deliverers are meeting on the Internet and swapping news, giving advice, scolding, kibitzing, and kvetching—all in writing.

Lousy writing. If the good news from cyberspace is that we're writing more, the bad news is that most of us aren't very good at it. Our words don't do justice to our ideas.

Computers haven't made us bad writers. We write badly because we don't know how. For many years, our schools have done a rotten job of teaching writing. Asking students to write without showing them how is like expecting them to drive before they've had a lesson. Still, it's never too late to improve. With practice, anyone who wants can write. Think of ballroom dancing: there's no shame in not knowing how, but there's no reason you can't learn. Sure, not everyone can be Fred Astaire or Ginger Rogers, but who wants to run backward down a flight of stairs, anyway (especially in high heels)?

Good writing is conspicuous by its absence. Even if you can't describe what it is, you know it when you *don't* see it, when what you're reading is tedious or blah or hard to follow. Good writing is writing that works. It makes sense. It's both comfy and elegant. It says just enough and no more. It has manners, not mannerisms. Good writing has all the right words—and not too many of them—in all the right places.

Sounds simple, doesn't it? Often it is. Merely adding or subtracting a single word can do wonders for a crummy sentence. Yet some writing is harder to fix; an idea may be missing, or stuck in the wrong place. There may be problems with logic, with tone, with rhythm. These problems, too, have solutions. Words fail all of us at one time or another. That's to be expected. If something comes too easily, it's probably not your best work.

You'll make mistakes, naturally. Who doesn't? Just as you don't expect perfection in everything you read, neither does the person you're writing for. No one has ever written anything perfect, although some have come mighty close. If you write honestly and do your best, most readers will give you the benefit of the doubt.

A final thought, for those of you with literary ambitions. Your favorite writers, and mine too, aren't without their faults. Trollope is fond of lengthy digressions, but we relish his Barsetshire novels nonetheless. Antonia Fraser's terrific history *The Wives of Henry VIII* is fascinating, but it has too damn many dashes. Melville's masterpiece, *Moby-Dick*, introduces interesting characters, only to drop them. I love rereading *Wuthering Heights*, though Emily Brontë's plot is ridiculously improbable. A writer can have faults and still be wonderful, because the best writing goes beyond simple mastery of language. Its power lies elsewhere—in one's understanding of the human heart and the ways of the world, in one's capacity for making moral judgments, in knowing a thing or two about life, in telling a great story.

So, I can hear you asking, if we aspire to greatness, why bother with the nuts and bolts? Well, the best writers may not follow every rule every time, but they follow most of them most of the time. And even if you're a Tolstoy or a Balzac, a Thurber or a McPhee, it doesn't hurt to learn the rules before you break them.

PART 1

Pull Yourself Together

Is Your Egg Ready to Hatch?

KNOW THE SUBJECT

Let's face it. Some subjects are harder to explain than others. A pipe organ is more complicated than a kazoo (even I can play Bach on the kazoo). No subject, though, is so complicated that it can't be explained in clear English. If you can't explain something to another person, maybe— just maybe—you don't quite understand it yourself.

Anything worth writing about is worth explaining. But you can't make something clear to someone else if it isn't clear to you. Before you write about a subject, make sure you know it inside and out. If there are questions in your mind, don't skip them or cover them up. Do your best to find the answers. Then, if questions remain, you can always be honest and say so; the reader will forgive you.

Whenever there's something wrong with your writing, suspect that there's something wrong with your thinking. Perhaps your writing is unclear because your ideas are unclear. Think, read, learn some more. When your egg is ready to hatch, it'll hatch. In the meantime, sit on it a bit longer.

The old admonition to "write what you know" is a cliché, but it's still good advice. No matter how vivid and fertile your imagination, you'll write best what you know best. Dr. Spock patted thousands of babies' bottoms, and generations of parents have turned to his venerable book on child care. Ben Hogan was the king of the swing, and his book on the fundamentals of golf has been a classic for years.

Speaking of classics, Melville and Conrad spent years at sea, and you can almost smell the salt air in their writing. In his rough-and-tumble youth, Dickens worked in a blacking factory, lived in the poorhouse, and clerked and ran errands in law offices and courts. Not surprisingly, his most lifelike characters aren't from high society. They're street people, beggars, thieves and spongers, laborers, petty clerks, and of course lawyers.

You may have noticed that in Jane Austen's novels, ladies are always present. What did the men say among themselves over their port when the women had withdrawn? Austen never took part in exclusively male conversation, so there is none in her novels. What's unfamiliar is kept offstage.

Not all of us have the luxury of writing only about what we know. A college student who's asked to write a paper on Kierkegaard can't very well decline and say he'd rather write about the Spice Girls. An ad executive with a fabulous wine cellar isn't likely to turn down the Bud account just because she thinks beer is déclassé. If you have to write about something unfamiliar, learn about it. Once you know the subject, you're ready to write.

You're probably wondering about those exceptions to the rule—writers who convincingly describe things they couldn't have seen with their own eyes. Anne Rice's *Interview with the Vampire* is vivid and convincing, even though she's never met one of the undead (at least, I hope she hasn't). She modeled the vampire Lestat after her blond husband, and set much of the atmospheric tale in her native New Orleans. Her writing comes alive because she's borrowed from what she knows in order to create a fictional world that's as real as the real thing.

Don't let the exceptions mislead you, though. An author who invents a world she hasn't seen, a reality she hasn't known, must be hellishly good to be believable. Most of us aren't hellishly good. We must know whereof we speak.

2

"The Party to Whom I Am Speaking"

KNOW THE AUDIENCE

A piece of writing requires at least two people: one to write it and one to read it. Who's going to read yours? It's important to ask, because people who don't know their readers or who forget about them aren't very good writers. You'll save yourself all kinds of trouble by learning this lesson early.

All writers, remember, are readers first. You'll read a lot more than you'll ever write. Let the reader in you influence the writer in you. Put yourself in the reader's place, then write what you'd like to read.

If the very idea of writing strikes fear into your soul, or if you freeze up when you start to write, you may have a problem imagining your reader. Fear of writing is often fear of the reader, especially one you don't know. And no wonder. Nothing is more daunting than an audience of strangers. Break the ice and get acquainted.

Similarly, if your writing is unfocused, your reader may be out of focus, too. When you can't see the target, you don't know where to aim. Sharpen your focus and bring the reader into the picture. Clarifying your audience will clarify your thinking and your writing.

All writing has an intended audience, even the telephone book (it may be monotonous, short on verbs, and heavy on numbers and proper nouns, but it sure knows its readers!). Your audience probably won't be as wide as your area code, but it could be almost anyone—your landlord, a garden club, the parole board, Internet jocks, a college admissions director, fiction readers, the editorial-page editor, the Supreme Court. Someone is always on the receiving end, but who? It's a big world out there, and before you write you have to narrow it down. Once you've identified your audience, everything you do—every decision you make about vocabulary, tone, sentence structure, imagery, humor, and the rest—should be done with this target, your reader, in mind.

Draw a mental picture of your reader and carry it with you as you write. Stop working now and then, and, like Lily Tomlin's telephone operator, ask, "Is this the party to whom I am speaking?"

Of course, you might have a different audience every time you write; where writing is concerned, one size does not fit all. As much as possible, try to anticipate your reader's needs, sophistication, likes and dislikes, attention span, mood, tastes, and sense of humor. In our personal relationships, this kind of discretion is called tact; in writing, it's called knowing your audience.

Here's how it works. Say you're writing a brochure for an investment firm, giving financial advice to the newly widowed. You'll want to sound serious but not gloomy, honest and direct but not intrusive. A wisecrack about the River Styx would not be appropriate. If you were advising college students, on the other hand, humor might be in order. Your tone and choice of words would be very different.

For better or for worse, audience is everything, no matter what you write. Unfortunately, some audiences seem to *require* bad writing: dullness (the phone book), pretentious language (an academic paper), hype (advertising copy). Take the academic paper, for example. Ask yourself who will be reading, then aim at that target. It may be that you hate pompous words like *syncretism* and *etiology*, and would rather use plain words like *joining* and *cause*. But since the professor or dissertation committee or scholarly journal expects gobbledygook and would reject anything else, you hold your nose and write "syncretism" and "etiology." If they want stuffy, give them stuffy. Once you're tenured or you're running the place, you can be yourself. (There's more on the pretentiousness problem in chapter 6.)

A fiction writer, too, should always imagine the people who'll be reading. I once saw a read-aloud children's book intended for preschoolers; each left-hand page had a picture and each right-hand page was packed with text, nicely written but impossibly long. The writer should have imagined the audience: a kid squirming in somebody's lap. While the grown-up drones on about the enchanted forest, the audience is clamoring to see the next picture.

You can't always hold the audience in your lap, even mentally. Unless you're writing to just one person, the audience will be made up of individuals, no two exactly alike. Still, they'll have certain things in common. Determine what those things are and keep them in mind as you write. You'll be surprised how much clearer your thinking and your writing will be. You may even make readers feel you're talking to each one alone.

While you're drawing your mental picture, remember that the readers are on your side (assuming you're not chewing them out). They want you to succeed. Why wouldn't they? When they read something, they want it to be good. Put mental smiles on their mental faces. You're not adversaries, after all. You're in this together, because you want to write something good and they want to read something good. Even someone who disagrees with what you say can enjoy reading it.

It's essential to imagine a friendly reader, because fear of your audience leads to serious problems. Writer's block is one of them, and so is first-person phobia; we'll get to them later. The fearful writer pictures the audience as a panel of Olympic judges, all holding up cards with 3's and 4's instead of 10's. But aside from editors, English teachers, and book critics, readers usually aren't sitting in judgment. They'll stay with you if you give them a nice move now and then—not every one has to be a triple axel.

Even though your mental picture of a friendly reader won't always be accurate, pretend it is. If you dislike the jerk you're writing for, don't show it. And don't imagine a reader lying in wait, ready to pounce on every little mistake, or your writing will sound defensive and fearful. Write as though you were addressing someone whose opinion you value, even if the reader is a boneheaded bureaucrat who wants to put a sewage treatment plant on your street, or a stingy insurance company that won't pay for your tummy tuck, or a neighbor who insists his boa constrictor loves children (as appetizers, maybe).

But be yourself as much as possible. If you're the serious type, be serious. Don't fake a breezy style or nudge readers with "Get it?" phrases. Assume they'll get it. Otherwise your writing will sound forced and artificial.

Don't talk down to a reader, either. Imagine he's intelligent, even if you know for a fact that he has a mind like a slotted spoon. It doesn't matter if the person who's going to read your paper is a cretin (or if, in the case of that children's book, the intended audience is three years old). Write as though you were addressing intelligent people you understand and respect. Don't patronize them, but don't talk over their heads. If something needs explaining, explain it.

Get to know your audience—use your imagination—because it's easier to give your best to someone you know and like. Think of your reader as a familiar presence, someone you can talk to. Your attitude will come through in your writing.

3

Get with the Program

THE ORGANIZED WRITER

This chapter is about organization. Yes, it's grunt work. And no, you may not skip to chapter 4. It doesn't matter how sloppy or tidy you are in real life. Even people whose closets look like Martha Stewart's can turn out writing that's a mess.

Unfortunately, organizing your mind isn't as simple as organizing your closet. You can't go to Home Depot or Hold Everything and buy the shelving and compartments and cubbyholes that will tidy your material and put it to work for you. Besides, when you put a closet in order, you throw things away. You never, ever throw away an idea.

Do I hear grumbling? Well, resign yourself to this part

of the process. It's not the part where you roll right along, humming a merry tune as the words tumble over one another in their eagerness to get on the page. Writers seldom shout, "Boy, this outline is really cookin'!" (Not that I recommend outlines, as you'll see.) What's more, the effort that goes into organization is largely invisible. You'll never hear a reader say, "My, this [essay/letter/novel/report] is beautifully organized." The job may be a pain in the butt, but it's thankless, too.

Now for the good news. Once you're organized, the rest becomes easier. No bogging down in the Great Grimpen Mire, that swampy wasteland pitted with the bones of lost writers whose last words were "Where am I?" You'll have a map. How do you get one?

First, you need something to organize: ideas, material, scraps of expertise, recipes, prognostications, anecdotes, scurrilous gossip, anything that might be relevant to what you want to write. And you get this stuff by hoarding it, by faithfully making notes and squirreling them away.

Let's say you're planning a magazine article about biker gangs. You could save a newspaper clipping about a turf war in Los Angeles, the nickname of a Hell's Angel you want to interview, or a tattoo ad from a biker magazine. Or perhaps you're writing a memo to your marketing manager about muffler sales in Toledo. You might jot down the boss's latest joke about Midas, or cut out an article from *Car & Driver* about auto emissions standards in Ohio.

Keeping a Stash

An idea in your head is merely an idle notion. But an idea written down, that's the beginning of something! Stripped down to its briefs, a piece of writing is nothing more than a handful of ideas, put into words and arranged to do a job. We all get ideas—try *not* thinking in the shower. The trick is to write them down.

How many inspirations have you gotten in the middle of the night, ideas that stole into your mind in the wee hours, only to steal away again by morning? "Great idea," you mumbled as you smugly went back to sleep, confident you'd remember that certain something, just what you needed for the writing project at hand. It might have been a snappy ending for the interoffice newsletter, a perfect first line for a poem to your beloved, a brilliant murder plot (fictional, we hope), or a dynamite punch line for the speech you promised to give at the chili supper.

Next time, write it down!

A writer with good material is one who never lets a useful nugget slip away. You can be sure that for every book you've read and loved, there once existed a pile of notes. Emily Brontë paused while cooking, ironing, or kneading dough to make notes for *Wuthering Heights*. Balzac was never without a notebook. Anatole France recorded his nighttime thoughts on pieces of paper that he let pile up under his bed. When that elusive phrase you've been seeking finally comes to mind, write it down. Do this without fail, no matter how inconvenient it is to stop what you're doing and write. (No! Don't take your hands off the wheel! Just do it as soon as you can.)

A tidbit doesn't have to be earth-shaking to be worth saving. It only has to be useful. It can be something that gives you a smile, a twinge, a pang, a shiver, a few goose bumps. It might be a word that grabs you because of its

sound or the images it evokes, or because it's your true
love's favorite expression. It could be a name, a scrap of
conversation, a magazine article, or simply a gesture, man-
nerism, or stray remark. If there's any chance you could
use it in the memo or paper you're planning, save it. And
when you make a note—this is important—add beside it
a word or two explaining why you wrote it. Your note
might look like this: "*symbiosis*—boss's favorite word." Or
"*schmooze*—add to job description." Without a little reminder, you'll forget why you made the note. I recently
came across a long-forgotten note of mine that said only
"Mahler." This must have meant something once, but I
can't remember what.

Make note-taking a habit. Carry with you a small notebook, a folded piece of paper, or a few file cards, and something to write with. This goes for the bedside table, too; add
a little keychain flashlight. Stick with one system. If you're
comfortable with file cards, stay with file cards, even if
some well-meaning person gives you a gorgeous, expensive
leather-bound journal. And keep the cards in the same
spot, so that reaching for them becomes automatic.

Once you've made a note—whether on a file card, a
page torn from a notebook, or a slip of paper—store it
in a handy place. This is your stash. Just as a farmer has
seed and a carpenter has lumber, a writer keeps a stash of
material—promising words or phrases, news clippings, or
idle notions.

The way you organize your stash depends on your
personality. If you're one of those systematic types—all
right, admit it—you might use an accordion file, with re-
lated notes neatly sorted by subject. My own notes tend to

accumulate like heaps of nuclear waste. Eventually they reach critical mass and I have to transfer them to manila folders just to get my desk back.

But no matter how you arrange your stash, don't make a fetish of it. You can be tidy later, when you start writing. And by all means, don't get too orderly and start throwing notes away (unless they say only "Mahler"). An interesting observation might not be relevant at the moment, but it could be perfect for some future writing project. Use it to start another stash.

Remember that the point of keeping a stash is to capture your ideas as they come. So for now, relax and don't be obsessive (just compulsive). This isn't work—not yet. It's pleasure.

Ages ago, when a childhood illness or a rainy day kept me inside, my mother used to let me play with her button box, an old fruitcake tin full of buttons in all sizes, shapes, and colors. Quite a few had been snipped from cast-off clothes and still had bits of fabric attached. Many were oddities: a big pink rhinestone, a carved wooden knot, the "eye" of a deceased bear. It was great fun to dump them out and arrange them in imaginative patterns. Sometimes I feel much the same pleasure in looking over a stash of notes before beginning to write.

But back to the project at hand. The organized writer does not digress!

The Third Degree

By now you have a healthy stack of usable material. Don't plunge into it right away, though; stop and think for a moment. Interrogate yourself: *What* do you want to say, *why* do you want to say it, and *how* do you want to say it? If you're not clear about these three things, take a walk— maybe a long one, or maybe only around the room—and think some more. And loosen up, for heaven's sake. You're just thinking.

Say the neighbors have chosen you to speak before the local zoning board about a proposed toxic dump the city wants to build on your block. For starters, give yourself the third degree: the what, the why, and the how. *What do you want to say?* The city should not build a toxic dump on my block. *Why do you want to say it?* Because we'll all turn green, property values will plummet, and there's a better spot across town. *How do you want to say it?* By presenting statistics on projected mortality rates, on residential re- sales in Chernobyl, and on the scarcity of registered voters living across town.

For the less civic-minded, here's another example. You're writing a magazine article about your grandmother on the occasion of her hundredth birthday. Again, run through the big three. *What do you want to say?* Gran is a specimen of living history, from the days of gaslight and horse-drawn carriages to space travel and cloning. *Why do you want to say it?* Because through the eyes of the elderly, we get a new perspective on the century. *How do you want to say it?* By using Gran's own words, along with old let- ters, diaries, and scrapbooks.

Even fiction should be subjected to the test. Suppose you want to write a short story about high school sweet- hearts who meet again at their fiftieth class reunion. *What do you want to say?* Former lovers look forward to re- kindling the old flame, but end up wondering what they ever saw in each other. *Why do you want to say it?* To show that puppy love isn't for grown-ups. *How do you want to say it?* By using his-and-hers remembrances of things past and present.

Flesh and Bones

Once you have the what, the why, and the how, you need a skeleton to hang your material on. Does this mean making an outline, one of those charts with Roman numerals and tiers of this, that, and the other? If you're comfortable with outlines, fine; make one. Some of my best friends are outline people. If you're not, here's a suggestion.

Draw up a list, which you may find less intimidating than a formal outline. We make lists all the time: lists of groceries, errands, correspondence, calls to answer. This is simply a list of the ideas you hope to get across or the points you want to include. Arrange the ideas in a logical order, one idea leading to the next.

What's a logical order? That depends on your material and your point of view. If your list of ideas is mostly a series of events, a straight chronological arrangement might work best. If you're building an argument, you might want to rank your ideas in order of importance. If you want to entertain in a speech or a light essay, you have to wow the audience at regular intervals, so spread the good stuff around and don't blow it all at once.

Perhaps you're giving a talk before the local garden club about repotting bonsai. If you choose a chronological approach, you might begin by talking about the first signs that the tree needs a transplant, then go on to picking a time, choosing a pot, pruning the roots, mixing new soil, and so on. If you want to build an argument, you might open by describing a pathetic, withered bonsai whose owner waited too long or ignored the danger signals. If you want to entertain, you might start by recalling how you were all thumbs (none of them green) the first time you repotted, but that the plant somehow survived the bungling.

Keep in mind that two different writers, given the same material, might organize it quite differently, yet just as effectively. There's no single answer to what makes a logical sequence. Pick one that makes sense to you, seems right for your material and your audience, and leads the reader smoothly from point to point.

If the items on your list don't readily fall into place, try this. Write them on sheets of paper, one item per sheet, with a word or two representing each item. Lay the sheets out—use the floor, if it helps, and invite Macavity to lounge somewhere else. Then arrange and rearrange the sheets into a chain of ideas, perhaps adding connecting items as links, until each idea naturally follows the one before and leads on to the next. Don't think sensational writing isn't put together this way. Ann Beattie used the floor to rearrange the parts of her novel *Picturing Will*. When F. Scott Fitzgerald wrote *This Side of Paradise* and *The Love of the Last Tycoon*, he covered the walls with charts showing the backgrounds and movements of his characters. And J. D. Salinger has been known to hang sheaves of notes from hooks mounted on the wall of his studio.

When you've put your ideas in order—you can get up off the floor now—take out your stash of notes and sort it. For each idea on your list, collect a pile of material (evidence, research, anecdotes, explanations) you might use to make that particular point. Steel yourself and put aside what doesn't belong. Sure, that bit about your seventh-grade homeroom teacher is a gem. But if it doesn't fit now, don't try to squeeze it in. Save it. There will be other days, other writing. Hoard your ideas like a miser.

You now have the bones of your piece (the list) and some of the flesh (the piles of relevant material). This framework is a guide to the size, scope, and structure of what you want to write, whether it's a short story, an office memo, a speech, a sermon, an essay, or a book.

As for the physical arrangement, or what you should have on your desk by now, that's up to you. You might make a chart listing the ideas in progression, with notations under each idea telling you which supporting materials to include. Or if you prefer, and if you have the space, arrange the piles in a neat row, one pile (labeled clearly) for each major idea on your list.

Expect your organization plan to stretch and change as you go along. It's *supposed* to. If it doesn't, there's something wrong. In the process of writing, you'll get ideas you weren't expecting. A hunch may come out of the blue, and suddenly you're off on an adventure. This phenomenon is called creativity, and your framework must inevitably change to accommodate it. A plan is supposed to help you write, and when it doesn't do that, it doesn't work. If you have to stand on your head to follow a blueprint, maybe the blueprint is upside down.

4

Commencement Address

THE FIRST FEW WORDS

Imagine you're on *Oprah*. The camera swivels your way, the red light is in your face, *you're on.*

What do you say? Your mouth opens, and out comes . . . "Uhhh, ahhh." The camera swivels away. In a split second, you've ruined your life!

Don't let this happen to you. Whether you're on camera or at the keyboard, get to it. Those first few words are your most important. They determine whether the audience will stick around for the rest.

An audience is a terrible thing to lose. Gorgeous writing, moving passages, clever wordplay, startling ideas—

they're all wasted if nobody reads far enough to find them. Avoid throwaway beginnings like these:

My purpose in writing this report on the plight of the takeout pizza industry is to show that . . .

I confess it's not without some trepidation that I turn to the subject of Elvis sightings, but . . .

At this point in time, you've no doubt observed that the frequent flyer . . .

The subject of this paper, potty training, has been the focus of considerable interest recently because . . .

It may be idle to speculate on the chances of a comet's destroying life on earth, and yet . . .

Needless to say, it's safe to assume that when we consider the rise of plastic wrap and the decline of waxed paper . . .

Generalities are hard to make, but my experience with alien abductions has been that . . .

After giving the subject of fat deprivation much thought, I can assert without fear of contradiction . . .

It's valuable to recall that only a few short years ago, the passenger pigeon was . . .

Eventually we all must acknowledge that the demographic impact of the station wagon . . .

Opinions to the contrary notwithstanding, it is distinctly possible that Jack the Ripper . . .

Don't start out by clearing your throat.

Now that you know what *not* to do, how do you find a beginning that works? The one you choose depends on your audience and on how you've decided to organize your piece. A meteorologist writing an article for the *Journal of Macromolecular Hermeneutics* wouldn't start out the same way as an Army chaplain planning a Memorial Day sermon or a stockbroker making a pitch to an investment club. Here are a few opening gambits.

Sum-Upmanship

One way to start your piece—as well as to get yourself writing—is to sum it up at the beginning. Write a short paragraph to tell the reader where you're going: *what* you plan to say, *why* it needs saying, and *how* you'll do it. A paper on Elizabethan drama might start this way: "Shakespeare's male-pattern baldness had a profound effect on his work. This revelation throws new light on his later plays, as a close examination of them will show."

Summarizing the what, the why, and the how (the third degree you gave yourself in the previous chapter) will help you start and keep you focused. In later drafts, this paragraph might move to another spot—after an opening anecdote, for example—or disappear altogether if it becomes unnecessary.

The summary beginning has been around for a long time, and it still works. In the fifth century B.C., Herodotus used this technique to begin his history of the Persian Wars. While the translation may have a few cobwebs, the opening sentence gets right to the point:

"These are the researches of Herodotus of Halicarnassus, which he publishes, in the hope of thereby preserving from decay the remembrance of what men have done, and of preventing the great and wonderful actions of the Greeks and the Barbarians from losing their due meed of glory; and withal to put on record what were their grounds of feud."

The writing still has grandeur, nearly twenty-five hundred years later.

You, too, can sum up the what, the why, and the how in your beginning. Just remember that a summary doesn't have to include the whole shebang. It only has to give the reader a taste of what's to come.

A Funny Thing Happened . . .

If you don't want to sum up your piece at the beginning, try starting with an anecdote. This technique can be overused, but everyone loves a good story, and a diversion or joke at the outset is a good way to catch the reader's attention. Keep it relevant, though. Starting off with a traveling-salesman joke, even an uproariously funny one, won't make much sense if your topic is periodontal disease. Use a joke about George Washington's dentures or Dracula's canines, or maybe a personal anecdote about flossing around that pesky upper-right bicuspid.

If you're writing an autobiography, a memoir, or something else about yourself, it may help to begin with an account of an important or symbolically significant incident in your life. Here's a bare-bones example: "If Mom hadn't sewn me a skeleton suit for Halloween when I was three, I never would have become the chiropractor I am today."

Anecdotal beginnings can work with almost any kind of writing, fiction or nonfiction. In the first paragraph of *Goodbye, Columbus,* Philip Roth gave us this unforgettable opening:

"The first time I saw Brenda she asked me to hold her glasses. Then she stepped out to the edge of the diving board and looked foggily into the pool; it could have been drained, myopic Brenda would never have known it. She dove beautifully, and a moment later she was swimming back to the side of the pool, her head of short-clipped auburn hair held up, straight ahead of her, as though it were a rose on a long stem. She glided to the edge and then was beside me. 'Thank you,' she said, her eyes watery though not from the water. She extended a hand for her glasses but did not put them on until she turned and headed away. I watched her move off. Her hands suddenly appeared behind her. She caught the bottom of her suit between thumb and index finger and flicked what flesh had been showing back where it belonged. My blood jumped."

You can almost feel the temperature rise. Who wouldn't keep reading?

Getting Physical

When a summary or an anecdote doesn't seem quite right, try a physical description of whatever you're writing about, whether a difficult client, the crime scene in a whodunit, or an archaeological dig.

Ernest Hemingway was especially good at this kind of beginning. Here's how he started a travel piece for a newspaper, years before he wrote his first novel:

"Switzerland is a small, steep country, much more up and down than sideways, and is all stuck over with large brown hotels built on the cuckoo clock style of architecture. Every place that the land goes sufficiently sideways a hotel is planted, and all the hotels look as though they had been cut out by the same man with the same scroll saw."

And this is how he began a 1923 interview with one of Lenin's aides:

"Georgi Tchitcherin comes from a noble Russian family. He has a wispy red beard and mustache, big eyes, a high forehead and walks with a slouch like an old clothes man. He has plump, cold hands that lie in yours like a dead man's and he talks both English and French with the same accent in a hissing, grating whisper."

Keep your antennae out when you read newspapers, and don't forget the sports pages. You'll find some of the best writing (and much of the worst) on your doorstep each morning.

Auspicious Beginnings

Readers are kindly for the most part. They'll forgive a clunky phrase or two later on if you win them over in the beginning. And when a beginning is good enough, it can win them for life. Here are some beginnings worth remembering.

"Whether I shall turn out to be the hero of my own life, or whether that station will be held by anybody else, these pages must show."

(Charles Dickens, *David Copperfield*)

"I was born a slave on a plantation in Franklin County, Virginia. I am not quite sure of the exact place or exact date of my birth, but at any rate I suspect I must have been born somewhere and at some time."
(Booker T. Washington, *Up from Slavery*)

"It was a bright cold day in April, and the clocks were striking thirteen."
(George Orwell, *Nineteen Eighty-four*)

"Philosophy, from the earliest times, has made greater claims, and achieved fewer results, than any other branch of learning."
(Bertrand Russell,
Our Knowledge of the External World)

"When Mrs. Frederick C. Little's second son was born, everybody noticed that he was not much bigger than a mouse. The truth of the matter was, the baby looked very much like a mouse in every way."
(E. B. White, *Stuart Little*)

"I can scarcely wait for the day of my imprisonment. It is then that my life, my real life, will begin."
(Elizabeth Bishop,
"In Prison," from *The Collected Prose*)

"Hale knew, before he had been in Brighton three hours, that they meant to murder him."

(Graham Greene, *Brighton Rock*)

"The problem lay buried, unspoken, for many years in the minds of American women. It was a strange stirring, a sense of dissatisfaction, a yearning that women suffered in the middle of the twentieth century in the United States. Each suburban wife struggled with it alone."

(Betty Friedan, *The Feminine Mystique*)

"What I am doing in Miami associating with such a character as Hot Horse Herbie is really quite a long story."

(Damon Runyon, "Pick the Winner")

"I was born in a house my father built."

(*The Memoirs of Richard Nixon*)

Memorable writing doesn't always start with a wow. Some of the novels I've most enjoyed lure the reader in more slowly: *Howards End, Women in Love, Hotel du Lac, The Death of the Heart, The Sheltering Sky, Excellent Women*, not to mention scores of nineteenth-century classics. But the leisurely beginning takes a kind of genius that most of us don't have and a kind of patience that most readers don't have, either. Our writing has to leave the starting gate quickly or we'll lose our audience.

You probably have a list of favorite writers. Take a look at some of the beginnings that have snagged you and kept you reading. Why do they work? What can you learn from them? If you read closely enough, you'll find ideas for your own writing. Don't steal, though, at least not outright. And please hold the clichés. "Once upon a time" was a good beginning . . . once upon a time.

From Here to Uncertainty

HOW AM I DOING?

Not bad. You've mastered your subject, you have a plan, you know your audience, and you've started to write. In the chapters to come, you'll pick up the skills—the fundamentals as well as the fancy moves—to make your writing the best it can be. Before we get to the tricks of the trade, though, there are a few things you should know about writing. I learned them the hard way, but you shouldn't have to.

Habit Forming

Everything you write, whether it's a shopping list, a Ph.D. thesis, or an e-mail giving directions to your house, will make a certain demand on your time. No matter what your project is, estimate how much time you'll need and then work out a writing schedule you can live with.

Let's use the shopping list as a no-frills example. You know you have to leave the house by three o'clock to do all your errands. And you know it'll take five minutes to scope out the refrigerator and the cupboards and the space under the sink and write down what you need to buy. So set aside five minutes sometime before three to do it. You procrastinators will need to stop whatever you're doing at two fifty-five. (By the way, the business about knowing your audience applies even here. If Aunt Millie is doing the shopping for you, write "peanut butter and jelly." If you're the intended reader, you can scribble "PB&J.")

You don't need me to tell you how to make a shopping list. The point is that everything you write will be better if you allow yourself the time to do it well. An autobiography would be a more challenging example. Say you'd like to finish it in five years, and you're willing to give it two hours every Sunday afternoon. By writing a page at each sitting, you'll end up with about 250 pages at the end of five years. If that length is in the ball park, and if you enjoy writing for two hours at a stretch, then your schedule is reasonable. But if you start fidgeting after an hour, change your schedule. Make your writing sessions shorter but more frequent, perhaps an hour on Saturday and an hour on Sunday. Or if you haven't lived all that much, write for just an hour a week and shorten your memoir by half.

Above all, take it easy with the schedule and keep your

expectations moderate, at least in the beginning. If you try to do too much you'll only disappoint yourself. If you find that you can easily do more, then give yourself more to do. Psychologically it's better to add to a schedule that's too light than to retreat from one that's too heavy. Why become discouraged right off the bat?

Once you've worked out a sensible schedule, stick to it. Do this whether you intend to make writing a daily habit or have to deliver a report a week from next Tuesday. Respect your routine and insist that others respect it, too. There's no need to be rude. Just tell friends and relatives you'll be working between this hour and that, and if they interrupt, you'll break their knees.

Whether you're in the mood or not, write when it's time to write. Don't wait around for inspiration. It almost never shows up punctually, believe me. I get my best ideas while I'm actually writing, and you probably will, too. Your engine will start out cold, but it'll warm up after a few laps.

One caution. You'll be amazed at how creative you become—not creative at writing, but creative at finding excuses not to write. I still fight this tendency. I can't find the word I want, for instance, or a paragraph won't come together. I stare off into space. Before I know it I've convinced myself that the windshield-wiper fluid in the car might be dangerously low and in the interest of public safety I'd better check it out—right now! Or in the course of looking something up in the dictionary, I'll come across the word "wheat" and realize that I've never baked bread. Never! It's something I've always wanted to try. And what better time than the present?

If making up excuses were an Olympic event, I'd win the gold medal every time, hands tied behind my back. Hey, that's not a bad idea. They made synchronized swimming an event, didn't they?

First-Draftsmanship

Classy prose does not leap, complete and fully formed, from anyone's typewriter or computer or quill pen. While it may read as naturally and eloquently as if it were flawless from the start and couldn't have been written any other way, don't believe it.

All writing begins life as a first draft, and first drafts are never (well, almost never) any good. They're not supposed to be. Expecting to write perfect prose on the first try is like expecting a frog to skip the tadpole stage.

Write a first draft as though you were thinking aloud, not carving a monument. If what you're writing is relatively short—a financial report, a book proposal, a term paper—you might try doing your first draft in the form of a friendly letter. The person at the other end could be someone real or imagined, even a composite reader.

Relax and take your time, but don't bog down, chewing your nails over individual words or sentences or paragraphs. When you get stalled (and you will), put down a string of X's and keep going. What you're writing now will be rewritten. If it's messy and full of holes, so what? It's only the first draft, and no one but you has to see it.

Accepting that your first draft is your worst draft can be extremely liberating. It's all right to sound like a jerk at this stage in the proceedings. Cut loose. Nobody's looking.

You wouldn't believe some of the rubbish that was in the first draft of this book—and I'll never tell.

But let's talk about you. Say you work in the marketing department of a fast-food chain with a big problem. There's a perception among the public that the company's products are radioactive. Your assignment is to come up with a campaign to convince people not only that the food is safe, but that it can add years to their lives and grow hair on bald heads. "Piece of cake," you tell the boss, rolling up your sleeves. Meanwhile, you're wondering where your next job will come from.

Stay calm. Approach the project as you would any other, even if this one seems impossible. Gather and organize your material—research by the Nuclear Regulatory Commission, testimonials from consumers, demographic studies, and so on. Then plunge into your first draft. If you like, dump in everything but the kitchen sink. This isn't a finished marketing proposal; you're only thinking aloud. Toss in your wildest inspirations. How about radiation-sensitive food wrappings that change color when emissions are present? Sure, include that. How about TV ads featuring a ninety-seven-year-old man with a full head of hair, wolfing down burgers as doctors check him over with Geiger counters? Get it on paper, on tape, or into the computer. Don't stop to examine ideas from every angle—just keep going.

Later, when you revise, you can agonize over the details and cut out the embarrassments. (Revision, the art of tinkering with what you've written, is worth a chapter in itself. In fact, it gets one: chapter 30.) In the meantime, nothing is too ridiculous for a first draft.

The Flexible Flyer

While you're writing you'll come up with ideas, or make discoveries, that can take you in new directions. "Jeepers, what a swell idea!" you'll say to yourself. Or maybe, "Duh! What took me so long?"

Sometimes, though, a sudden inspiration or some eye-popping information won't fit neatly into your grand design, the organization plan we talked about in chapter 3. What to do?

Even the best-laid plan can't anticipate every brain wave. When a glowing lightbulb appears over your head, don't turn it off. A good idea is a gift, not an inconvenience. If your writing plan doesn't let in any light or leave room for a fresh idea, then change it. It's supposed to make writing easier, not harder.

Imagine that you're writing a laudatory essay about your great-uncle Klaus, who died before you were born. He emigrated from Berlin to Brazil toward the end of World War II, and you've organized your material around his many philanthropies on behalf of the Amazon Indians. Halfway through the project, you come across old documents that explain why he left Berlin in such a hurry, and how he acquired that old SS uniform in the trunk. I'd say it's time to revise your writing plan.

Flexibility is a skill every writer should develop. If the human mind weren't flexible, we'd still be living in caves.

Faith, Hope, and Clarity

I'll always take a plain sentence that's clear over a pretty one that's unintelligible. When your writing is hard to understand, it's just so much slush, no matter how many beautiful images and nice rhythms it has. Readers won't like what they can't understand. They may understand it and still not like it, certainly. But that's a chance you have to take.

The best writing is the clearest; we sense its meaning immediately. The subject—particle physics, perhaps—may be over our heads, but the writing should never be. Albert Einstein was able to convey difficult scientific ideas simply and elegantly. "I think that a particle must have a separate reality independent of the measurements," he wrote. "That is, an electron has spin, location and so forth even when it is not being measured. I like to think that the moon is there even if I am not looking at it."

No subject is so complicated that it can't be explained clearly and simply. Of course, simplicity is deceptive. Turning out flashy, dense, complicated prose is a breeze; putting things down in simple terms that anyone can understand takes brainwork. Still, you don't have to be an Einstein to write well. When you reach the inevitable impasse, try another approach. Every time you do this, consider it a step forward, not back.

Take Five

Some people don't know when to stop. But resting is part of the job. Like Bertie Wooster's beloved oolong, it restores the tissues. A rest can take many forms, from a simple mental pause to a walk around the room to calling it a day. For those of you who haven't already figured this one out, here's when to give yourself a break.

- **When you're indecisive.** If you find yourself staring at the computer screen for ten or fifteen minutes, going back and forth between two trifling choices until neither seems better or worse than the other, stop. You've lost your perspective.

    Maybe you're writing a whodunit and can't decide whether the detective is "stunning" or "gorgeous." Quit futzing around. Take a breather, go back and make a choice, then move on to more important things.

- **When you start seeing double.** If the page or the computer screen begins to blur even though you've just gotten new glasses, call a time-out. Not many writers do their best when they're tired.

- **When you can't concentrate.** If you're unable to tune out the hum of traffic or ignore the neon sign across the street, a brief rest might be in order. Be honest, though, and make sure you genuinely can't concentrate even if you try. There's a thin line between truly lacking concentration and simply looking for excuses not to write.

- **When your brain is fried.** My brain gives out after about four hours of writing. If I try to go on, I become incoherent. Some people can write from dawn to dusk, some for only an hour or two; everyone has a limit. When you've reached yours, quit for the day.

- **When you're feeling lousy.** If you can't think of anything but your aching head, your stuffy si-

nuses, or your 103-degree fever, maybe you should
be in bed.

- **When your writing stinks.** If your work is going
badly and everything you do only makes it worse,
stop for a while. You may need to end your writing session early. Next time, take a fresh look, try
a new approach.

When you quit, however, don't immediately start
doing something you enjoy, like taking a nap or dashing to
the fridge for some Ben & Jerry's. Instead, do some unpleasant task, like paying bills. Don't reward behavior that
you shouldn't encourage.

I find that when my work stalls, things look much better the next day. Time and distance can work wonders.

Talking of Michelangelo

If you think that your prose is deathless, that what you're
writing is the literary equivalent of the Sistine Chapel,
scrape yourself off the ceiling. It may be as good as you
think, but chances are it's not quite that fabulous and you
need to come down off your high.

The buzz you get when you're really on is one of the
great rewards of writing, yet it feels very much like the
buzz you get when you're deceiving yourself. By all means
enjoy your dizzy euphoria. Just remember to take another
look after your head clears. Try to see your work as a
reader would, coming to it cold, and don't be crushed if it's
less dazzling the second time around. Self-intoxication is
dangerous only if you fail to sober up.

Signs of Progress

Remember Sisyphus, the Greek character who was con-
demned to roll a stone uphill, only to have it roll down
again? He ought to be the patron saint of writers. Any
writing project, even a small one, seems a Sisyphean task if
you feel you're going nowhere—a common feeling among
writers.

Sometimes, though, you'll think you're going nowhere
when in fact you've almost arrived. That's because progress
seldom announces itself. It comes in increments, without
orchestral accompaniment, so don't think you're toiling in
vain because you don't hear a flourish of trumpets every
time you write. When you learn to recognize signs of
progress, you won't feel you're running in place. Here are
some signs to look for. Don't expect to see them all. Even
one can keep you going.

- **You've met your quota.** If you've set a quota—a
  number of words or pages you hope to produce
  each time you write—you have a built-in progress
  meter. If you don't have a quota, and if you work
  on a computer, do a word count at the end of each
  session. I do this every time I write, if only to
  watch the numbers change. When the count
  grows, that's progress. When the count shrinks,
  that can be progress, too—if I've cut out something dumb.
- **You've done your time.** Even if you haven't written very much at a sitting, at least you've started
  on time, finished on time, and done some think-

ing in between. Keeping to a schedule is definitely progress.

- **Your writing holds up.** If it still looks good to you the next day, it probably is.
- **You can't wait to get back to work.** Now you're getting somewhere.
- **You can't stop.** Let's not kid ourselves. No one feels like this every day.
- **You're not afraid to show your writing.** If you have the confidence to ask for someone else's opinion, you've made progress.
- **You can take criticism without collapsing.** Well, you asked for it, didn't you? Besides, if criticism helps you get your project back on track, that's progress. (If only I could follow my own advice!)

The Payoff

When you read something you love, something so beautiful and right and true that it leaves you breathless with admiration, you probably think, "Words come easy to her," or "His writing is effortless." That's what writers want you to think. But the effortless feel of good writing takes effort to achieve. As Samuel Johnson put it, "What is written without effort is in general read without pleasure."

Don't think that what's hard for you comes naturally to others. Everyone has to work at writing well. But there's a payoff—two payoffs, actually.

First, the techniques for writing well aren't hard to learn. And they work! You'll find them in the chapters ahead, the fundamentals and then the fine points.

Second, effort really does make a difference. If you work at your writing, even a little, you'll see results. You may not use every bit of advice in this book, but any improvement at all is worth the trouble. Remove only one word of jargon, sharpen only one fuzzy idea, goose only one sentence with a livelier verb, and your writing will be that much better.

PART 2

The Fundamental Things Apply

fyugfnfewyendjfmocfsjetwnfkfdofffefndtwykt
jghrtgerfdtsyhejuogehtrysfertdgwrsteyhfushkey
dhtjncgeebjduwournhrsgeyifkdleystqnnaqmmxusdni
jste 6 feujnflksmcdafewdurheksjfredhulisfd
fryusfetrdgshuwyrtghsyeturheydfgj
hrtegsfdytjhrjuktjfgersfegydthmburfdgsyegfhsuyefo

Pompous Circumstances

HOLD THE BALONEY

This has happened to me, and I'm sure it's happened to you. You're listening to people talk, at a board meeting or a seminar or a discussion group or even at some la-di-da cocktail party, and everyone is being *soooo* impressive. The pretentious language gets deeper and deeper, until you're up to your knees in big words and bureaucratic/academic/corporate gobbledygook.

Just as you're thinking you'd rather be somewhere else, a voice of reason pipes up with a simple question or comment that cuts through the baloney:

"Yes, but does it work?"

Or: "By 'eggplant' you mean purple."

Or: "In other words, we're fired."

Refreshing, isn't it?

If this were a better world, everyone would write and speak simply and clearly all the time. Unfortunately, we're not always comfortable with the audience or the subject. When we're insecure—perhaps we don't know enough, we don't trust our understanding, or we're trying to impress—we resort to pretentious language. We tart up our writing with authoritative-sounding twaddle: inflated words, jargon, the phrase of the moment. The way to sound authoritative is to know your subject (there I go again), not to camouflage your weaknesses with big words. It takes a knowledgeable writer to use simple language, to "eschew surplusage," as Mark Twain said.

Allow me, therefore, to suggest that hereafter you utilize the optimum downsizing in terminology. Translation: Use plain words. If you're a commodities trader and it's raining, say it's raining. Don't say that corn futures are up because *predictions of increased precipitation have in the present instance proved accurate.* If you're a teacher and little Jeremy can't add, tell his mom that he has trouble with arithmetic, not that *his computational skills do not meet his age-expectancy level.* Keep your words few and simple.

I'm not saying it's never appropriate to use heaps of big words, even extra-extra-large ones. But when simple English will do as well, why dress up an idea in ribbons and bows? They only obscure the message. If your object is to communicate, don't let anything come between you and the reader.

Sometimes it takes courage to drop our pretensions,

to choose *use* instead of *utilize*, *rain* instead of *precipitation*, *arithmetic* instead of *computational skills*. An idea expressed in simple English has to stand on its own, naked and unadorned, while ostentatious words sound impressive even when they mean nothing.

Not all pompous writers are showing off or covering up their ignorance. Some are just timid, imagining that their ideas are flimsy or flawed or silly, even when they aren't. If you've done your homework, you shouldn't have to disguise your ideas with showy language. Be brave. Write plainly.

The truth about big, ostentatious words is that they don't work as well as simple ones. Here's why:

- Pretentious words are mushy, because they're often more general and less specific than simple, concrete ones. *Precipitation* could mean snow or sleet as well as rain. *Computational skills* could mean addition or subtraction or the ability to use an abacus.
- Big words are less efficient than small ones. Why use a shotgun when a flyswatter will do?
- Bureaucratese is easier to misinterpret. Look at the problems diplomats and politicians have understanding one another. (Everyone who uses the word *parameter*, for example, seems to mean something different.)
- Show-off words have a patronizing air, as if the writer were talking down to the reader. "My vocabulary is bigger than yours," the stuffed shirt might as well be saying. "I'm an insider and you're not."

All right, I wasn't born yesterday. I can hear the protests mounting, especially from the corridors of business and academia: "Are you nuts? If I use simple language, I'll sound like a blockhead. In my field, you have to use lots of jargon. Everyone does it."

True. At times we have to play the game, to use language that's stuffier than we'd like. Until we can make the rules ourselves, we play along. A marketing specialist might have to write: "Demographic data as well as experience with selective focus groups indicate that initial product response will be more favorable than the performance-based patterns demonstrated by recidivist consumers." The boss doesn't want the simple truth: "They'll buy it until they learn it doesn't work."

So what do you do? If you can't always cut the baloney and write in plain English, just do it whenever you can. Choose the simple, concrete word over the mushy, complicated one every chance you get. Believe me, ninety-nine readers out of a hundred are reasonable people who would rather be informed than impressed. They're grateful for clear, straightforward writing, and they'll remember it longer. Tell them what they need to know and let them get on with their lives.

Simplicity takes practice, oddly enough, because pretentiousness is contagious. We tend to absorb the words we hear around us, and many professions have become industries for cranking out flatulent language. A sociologist used to psychobabble (*gender reassignment*, for instance) will find it hard to write plainly (*sex change*). But simplicity is worth the effort, so here are some of the pretensions you should learn to recognize and avoid.

- **Mushy words.** Stay away from vague or evasive language, especially euphemisms such as *technical adjustment* instead of *market drop*, *gaming* instead of *gambling*, *collateral damage* instead of *civilian casualties*, *pre-owned* instead of *used*. Vague expressions like these blur meaning in hopes of making distasteful ideas more palatable.

- **Windbaggery.** Don't inflate your writing with bureaucratic hot air. A windbag uses a puffed-up phrase like *ongoing highway maintenance program* when he means *roadwork*. He says *recreation specialist* when he means *gym teacher*.

- **Artificial sweeteners.** Avoid officialese that hides or sweetens an unpleasant reality. It may be good public relations to say *fatalities* instead of *deaths*, or *terminated* instead of *fired*, but it's wishy-washy English. And let's not forget *plausible deniability*, from the days before *spin control*.

- **Cool words.** If you expect your writing to outlast yesterday's mashed potatoes, try not to use the fashionable word, the cool expression that's on everybody's lips. Like last year's hemlines, they get old fast. Trendy expressions ("Get out of my face"; "Quit busting my chops") don't wear well, but plain language ("Go away"; "Don't bother me") has staying power. Be warned that hip terms are contagious. They sneak up on you. Before you know it, you're using them, too. That's not cool.

- **Affectations.** Steer clear of foreign, technical, or scientific terms if you don't need them. Unless it's appropriate to do otherwise, use simple English.

Instead of *comme il faut*, try *proper*; instead of *potable*, try *drinkable*; instead of *Rana catesbeiana*, try *bullfrog*. Between us—not *entre nous*—plain English is better.

- **Empty words.** Beware of meaningless phrases that cover up a naked fact—the Emperor has no clothes. That is, the writer just doesn't know. Often the unintelligible hides behind the unpronounceable. A puzzled art history major might write: "Within the parameters of his creative dynamic, the artist has achieved a plangent chiaroscuro that is as inchoate as it is palpable, suffusing the observer with mystery." That sounds more self-assured than "Beats me." Unless you're hiding the fact that you don't know what's going on, write plainly.

- **Stretch limos.** Don't use words that are longer than they have to be. Shorter is usually better. Some writers (among them lawyers, doctors, and scientists) may need long words to be precise. But others (academics, politicians) often seem to use them just to make an impression. A scholar recently had this to say about Freud's writing habits: "Drafts embody the second stage of the dynamic that characterizes the genesis of Freud's texts." In other words, "The second thing he did was make a draft." Unless your audience absolutely demands big words, have the courage not to use them.

Not long ago, Alan D. Sokal, a physics professor at New York University, showed that even the most absurd statements will be swallowed whole if they're concealed in obscure and pretentious language. He wrote an article, published as serious scholarship by an academic journal, in which he said: "It has thus become increasingly apparent that physical 'reality,' no less than social 'reality,' is at bottom a social and linguistic construct; that scientific 'knowledge,' far from being objective, reflects and encodes the dominant ideologies and power relations of the culture that produced it; that the truth claims of science are inherently theory-laden and self-referential; and consequently, that the discourse of the scientific community, for all its undeniable value, cannot assert a privileged epistemological status with respect to counter-hegemonic narratives emanating from dissident or marginalized communities."

Pretty impressive! But what did he mean? Simply that there's no real world. We made it up. Yet no one realized this preposterous article was a gag until Sokal himself fessed up.

The most essential gift for a good writer, Hemingway wrote, is a built-in, shock-proof baloney detector. (No, he didn't use the word "baloney.") So develop a detector of your own and keep it in good working order. Know windbaggery and artificial sweeteners and all the rest when you see them. Then write without them.

7

The Life of the Party

VERBS THAT ZING

Here's to the verb! It works harder than any other part of the sentence. The verb is the word that gets things done. Without a verb, there's nothing happening and you don't really need a sentence at all. So when you go shopping for a verb, don't be cheap. Splurge.

Because verbs are such dynamos, writers often take them for granted, concentrating their creativity on the nouns, adverbs, and adjectives. This is a big mistake. Find an interesting verb and the rest of the sentence will practically take care of itself. Controlled studies have shown conclusively that a creative verb generates twice the energy of a noun of equal weight and density, and three times that of an adjective or adverb. Trust me. I've got the figures here somewhere.

Learn to spot provocative verbs. Newspapers are a good source. A friend of mine is a particularly colorful writer, and I often wondered how she came up with such sparklers. One day she told me. "I read the sports pages and collect interesting verbs like 'pummel' and 'clobber' that I religiously copy into a little notebook." She reconsiders every verb she's written, then replaces the dull ones.

How can you detect a dull verb? Your nose knows. Take a whiff. If a sentence has a musty smell, there's a stale verb lurking somewhere—in a cliché (*Intel **plays** hardball*), in a predictable or routine phrase (*A shot **rang** out*), or maybe in a passive guise (*He **was given** an A* instead of the active and more forceful *He **got** an A*). Passive verbs, by the way, are often a symptom of indirect writing. There's more about how to protect yourself from this highly communicable disease in chapter 21.

English is a vast, rich language, packed with interesting verbs. Use them. I'm not saying you should sit with *Roget's Thesaurus* at your side, plucking out wacky, eccentric verbs and shoehorning them into every one of your sentences. Just try a juicy verb once in a while.

Interesting verbs are easy to recognize: they're fresh or unusual; a small surprise now and then grabs the reader's attention. They're active (I'll talk about the exceptions later). And they're strong.

The strong ones are more than interesting—they're economical. They don't need to be propped up with extra words. Weak verbs need help (*The stockholders **asked insistently**; The detective **walked with a swagger***), but strong ones support themselves (*The stockholders* **insisted**; *The detective* **swaggered**). So if you spot too many props in your writing—adverbs like *insistently* and prepositional phrases like *with a swagger*—replace them with stronger verbs.

Rooting out wussy verbs is an excellent way to start revising your work. (There's more about revision in chapter 30.) For instance, it's been my experience that *experience* is a mighty weak verb. Replace it if you can—and you nearly always can. In the handwritten draft of one of his lectures on literature, Vladimir Nabokov crossed out the word, changing "experience that magic" to "bask in that magic." Notice how the stronger verb illuminates the phrase.

As for passive verbs, before condemning them I'll offer a word or two in their defense. You might prefer them in these situations:

- When it's not important to say who did something: *The merchandise* **was stowed** *in the cargo hold*.
- When you'd rather not say who's responsible: *My homework* **has been lost**.
- When you don't know whodunit: *Norman's manuscript* **was stolen**.
- When you want to delay the punch line: *Julia* **was done in** *by a spinach soufflé*.

In most cases, though, a passive verb sits there like a plaster Buddha, one step removed from the action. The sentence *Their meal* **was eaten** *in three hours* is a snooze. You can hear the clock slowly ticking.

An active verb has more energy, more buzz; it gets to the point sooner and with fewer words. The sentence *They ate for three hours* has blood in its veins, not embalming fluid. You can imagine hungry people gobbling and snarfing. Life, my dear, is being lived, if I may be allowed a passive verb.

teguginiewyendjrmocisjetwnikidofiierndtwy
ftjghrtgerfdtsyhejuogehtrysfertdgwrsteyhfushk
vgdhtjncgerehiduwournhrsgeyifkdleystqnnaqmmxusd
epjsteff   eujnflksmcdafewdurheksjfredhulis
ylryusfetrdgshuwyrtghsyeturheydfg
jfhrtegsfdytjhrjuktjfgersfegydthmburfdgsyegfhsuy

8

Call Waiting

PUTTING THE SUBJECT
ON HOLD

I can't stand call waiting, an annoying necessity at our house. I get discombobulated when I have to interrupt one conversation and start another, and maybe even another, then try to pick up where I left off.

Sentences can be confusing and disorienting, too. The subject is mentioned early on, then comes some other stuff, and maybe some other stuff, and by the time the verb shows up we've forgotten who's on hold. Putting a subject too far from the verb is asking the reader to take another call in mid-sentence.

Here's what happens when a verb falls too far behind: *Taking up his meerschaum, Holmes, secure in the knowledge that Moriarty's goose was cooked, popped it into his mouth.* That's a confusing sentence, and not because it's too long. It's disorienting because the subject (*Holmes*) is too far from the verb (*popped*). What did Holmes do? We assume he put the pipe into his mouth, but for all we know, he might have popped the goose into Moriarty's.

The solution is to bring the actor (*Holmes*) and the action (*popped*) closer together: *Taking up his meerschaum,* **Holmes popped** *it into his mouth, secure in the knowledge that Moriarty's goose was cooked.* The sentence is just as long, yet there's no way to misread it.

If putting subject and verb close together is so easy and works so well, why do writers separate them? Perhaps they think it's less clunky to cram a lot of information in the middle of a sentence than to tack it on either end. Not true. Most of the time, it's smoother and clearer to put extra information at the front or the back than to lump it in the middle.

Even when we understand a sentence, we can often improve it by moving the subject and verb closer together. Keep your eye on the actor and the action in this example: **Drew,** *seriously ticking off the personal trainer who was helping her drop twenty pounds for her role as a bulimic princess,* **ate** *a whole quart of Cherry Garcia.*

If this sounds awkward, it's because we have to wait so long to find out what happened. There's too much information crammed in between the actor (*Drew*) and the action (*ate*). By the time we learn what Drew did that was so off-ticking, we've had a bit of a workout ourselves. Now let's put the doer next to what's being done: **Drew ate** *a whole quart of Cherry Garcia, seriously ticking off the*

personal trainer who was helping her drop twenty pounds for
her role as a bulimic princess.

That's still a mouthful, but isn't it better? By keeping
subject and verb near each other, you're dealing with one
idea at a time. You aren't asking the reader to take another
call, to put a thought on hold while you interrupt with
more information.

There's a bonus here that goes beyond the sentence.
Once you get into the habit of avoiding digressions on a
small scale, you'll be able to spot them in larger chunks
of writing. Just as the parts of a sentence sometimes get
separated or out of order, so do the ideas that hold together paragraphs, chapters, even whole books. Hold that
thought.

egug iniewyend jimoeis jetwhikidoiieindtwykt
ighrtgerfdtsyhejuogehtrysfertdgwrsteyhfushkey
dhtjnege hiduwournhrsgeyifkdleystqnnaqmmxusdni
jste   teujnflksmcdafewdurheksjfredhulisfd
l ryusfetrdgshuwyrtghsyeturheydfgj
hrtegsfdytjhrjuktjfgersfegydthmburfdgsyegfhsuyefc

9

Now, Where Were We?

A TIME AND A PLACE FOR EVERYTHING

Did you ever wake up in the middle of the night, maybe while traveling or on vacation, and wonder where you were and what day it was? That's the feeling readers have when they can't tell where or when something is happening.

And when more than one thing is happening, the confusion multiplies. Take this sentence, please! *The director of technology announced that several employees were abusing their Internet privileges Tuesday at the staff meeting.*

Excuse me? Did the chief techie say this at the staff meeting? Or was that where the hanky-panky took place? And goodness, look at the time. What happened Tuesday? The cybercrime or the announcement?

When we write, we often take such details as time and place for granted because they're obvious to us. They won't be obvious to the reader, though. This version clears things up: *At Tuesday's staff meeting, the director of technology announced that several employees were abusing their Internet privileges.* Simply by moving the time and the place, we leave no doubt about what happened on Tuesday, and where.

The Space–Time Conundrum

Even when there's only one thing happening, a sentence can be confusing if the time or place is unclear. Readers won't know where is there and when is then. Here's an example of fuzzy timing that you might find in an investment newsletter: *Our technical analysts predicted the stock market correction last week.*

What happened last week, the prediction or the correction? Be clear. Make it: *Last week our technical analysts predicted the stock market correction.* Or: *Our technical analysts predicted last week's stock market correction.*

When a reader is lost in space, a simple sentence can be simply maddening. What's the poor reader to make of this one? *Buck lectured about the typhoon in Dublin.*

Was the typhoon in Dublin, or is that where Buck gave the lecture? The last I heard, Ireland wasn't in the tropics, so make it: *In Dublin, Buck lectured about the typhoon.* Or: *Buck lectured in Dublin about the typhoon.*

The Misplaced Reader

Words that help point us in the right direction (prepositions such as *on, about,* and *around*) sometimes give confusing signals. The reader might take an unnecessary detour or even a wrong turn. Notice how the preposition *on* can give a sentence two very different meanings: *Jon wrote a book on Mount Everest.*

Is Mount Everest the subject of the book? Or is that where Jon wrote it? You could clear up the confusion by using a clearer signal: *Jon wrote a book about Mount Everest.* Or if Jon likes to write in thin air, you could move the mountain: *On Mount Everest, Jon wrote a book.*

Here are two more examples of how crossed signals can send readers in the wrong direction:

The mouse ran around the clock. If the mouse ran non-stop, say so. If the mouse circled the clock, write it that way.

There were rumors about the dormitory. Was the dorm the subject of the rumors? Or were the rumors spreading through the dorm? Say it one way or the other.

Infinitive Wisdom

Time and place sometimes go astray when a sentence has two or more verbs and one of them is an infinitive (a verb that's usually preceded by *to*). This example could be read in two ways: *Alec asked Kim to marry him in the Jacuzzi.*

Did Alec propose in the Jacuzzi, or is that where he wants to get married? (Stranger things have happened.) Unless he wants a wedding in a whirlpool, make it: *In the Jacuzzi, Alec asked Kim to marry him.* Better yet: *Alec proposed to Kim in the Jacuzzi.*

This sentence could also be read in two ways: *Aunt Agatha threatened to disinherit Bertie when she caught him gambling.*

Did she threaten Bertie *when* she caught him? Or *if* she caught him? Make it: **When** *Aunt Agatha caught Bertie gambling, she threatened to disinherit him.* Or: *Aunt Agatha threatened to disinherit Bertie* **if** *she caught him gambling.*

Every Now and Then

Some of the words we use to tell us when and where— *here, there, now, then, this,* and *that*—can leave readers scratching their heads. If these words are used carelessly, readers can't tell where is here and when is now.

In a letter to the local library board, you might find a sentence like this: *Since the new branch is so popular and the main library is underused, it is* **here** *we should spend our resources.* What does the writer mean? Should the bucks go to the new library, or the old one? In other words, where is *here*?

The writer might mean this: *Since the new branch is so popular, it is* **here** *we should spend our resources, not on the underused main library.* Or this: *Since the main library is underused, it is* **here** *we should spend our resources, not on the popular new branch.* Those sentences may not be graceful, but their meaning is obvious. When *here* or *there* could refer to more than one place, rearrange the sentence to make clear which place you mean. Otherwise the reader will be nowhere.

We can run into the same sort of trouble with *now* and *then.* Here's part of an e-mail that an insurance agent might receive after a fender bender: *The roads were slippery even before the rain turned to sleet, and it was* **now** *the car began to skid.* When is *now*? Did the car start to skid before or after the rain turned to sleet?

Here's one interpretation: *The roads were slippery and it was **now** the car began to skid, even before the rain turned to sleet.* Here's another: *The rain turned to sleet on the slippery roads, and it was **now** the car began to skid.*

Two more words, *this* and *that*, can also be used to indicate time and place. And like the others, they can be misread: *The Hotel Pierre is in the East Sixties, and **this** is where she'd like to stay.* Where is *this*? In the hotel, or in the neighborhood?

We can clear things up by dropping *this*: *The Hotel Pierre is in the East Sixties, where she'd like to stay.* Or: *She'd like to stay at the Hotel Pierre, which is in the East Sixties.*

Incidentally, these words (*here* and *there*, *now* and *then*, *this* and *that*) can trip you up in other ways, as well. For more on them, and on other kinds of illogical writing, see chapter 17.

As is often the case, what's good for a single sentence is good for the whole enchilada. Get used to thinking about time and place with each sentence you write. Then you'll be less likely to muddle the larger picture. You'll keep the wheres and the whens straight from paragraph to paragraph, section to section, chapter to chapter.

Now, where was I?

The It Parade

PRONOUN PILEUPS

How about *it*? And while we're at *it*, let's talk about *us*—also *he*, *she*, *him*, *her*, *they*, and a slew of similar words, the small conveniences that refer to things or people we'd rather not mention by name.

These words are called pronouns because they're substitutes for nouns (*pro* means "for" or "in place of"). Most of the time we can decipher the shorthand and figure out what *it* is and who *they* are. When the words in a sentence are in the right order, there's no doubt about *it*. Even when the word order is iffy, logic and context usually help us fill in the blanks—but don't count on it.

This sentence leaves no doubt: *The La-Z-Boy is moth-eaten, so Homer's replacing it.* Here, *it* can only mean the La-Z-Boy.

Add another noun, though, and the shorthand is blurry: *The upholstery on the La-Z-Boy is moth-eaten, so Homer's replacing it.* Is *it* the La-Z-Boy or the upholstery? Will the mystery noun please stand up? You might mean this: *The upholstery is moth-eaten, so Homer's replacing the La-Z-Boy.* Or this: *The La-Z-Boy is moth-eaten, so Homer's replacing the upholstery.*

It is one of those creepy-crawly words that sneak up on writers. Every time you write *it*, imagine a reader asking, "What is *it*?" If *it* isn't obvious, either ditch it or rearrange the words.

Be careful with sentences like this, with two or more nouns in front of an *it*: *Philippe kept his opinion of the painting to himself until it became popular.* Until what became popular, the painting or his opinion? Make sure the reader knows what *it* is. Try this: *Until the painting became popular, Philippe kept his opinion of it to himself.* Or in case he's an art critic: *Until his opinion of the painting became popular, Philippe kept it to himself.*

If you'll pardon the déjà vu all over again, here's one more example: *Yogi's book about the World Series was sold even before it was completed.* Before what was completed, the book or the World Series?

One way to fix the sentence is to drop *completed* and use a more precise verb that clears away the fog: *Yogi's book about the World Series was sold even before it was written.* Another solution is to add *he*, making clear who did *it*:

Yogi's book about the World Series was sold even before he completed it.

Who's Who

If one shorthand word can gum up a sentence, imagine what a whole pack can do. Try to identify the pronouns in this pileup: *Fred told Barney he'd ask a neighbor to feed **his** pterodactyls, but **he** forgot, **they** died, and now **they** aren't speaking.*

Whose pterodactyls? Who forgot what? Who (or what) died? Who's not speaking to whom? When you use pronouns, you know the cast of characters. Readers won't know and shouldn't have to guess. This might be what the writer means: *Fred said he'd ask a neighbor to feed Barney's pterodactyls, but the neighbor forgot, the pets died, and now Fred and Barney aren't speaking.* It's not elegant, but at least we know who did what.

Even a short sentence can be confusing if it has a mystery pronoun: *Duke said Boomer broke **his** nose.* Since two guys are mentioned, we don't know whose nose was broken—Boomer's or Duke's. If Boomer took the blow, we could write: *Duke said Boomer broke **his** own nose.* If Duke's face was rearranged, we might say: *Duke said **his** nose was broken by Boomer.* (A passive verb comes to the rescue.)

Those solutions aren't as economical as the original sentence, but clarity comes first. Sometimes we can solve a pronoun problem by using a different verb altogether: *Duke **accused** Boomer of breaking **his** nose.*

Oh, one more thing about fuzzy pronouns. Don't substitute *the former* and *the latter* to make your meaning clear (*Duke said Boomer broke **the latter's** nose*). The result is annoying and pretentious. A good rule of thumb is to avoid the kind of pompous language used by people you'd like to punch in the nose.

11

Smothering Heights

MISBEHAVING MODIFIERS

Mrs. Trotter, my fourth-grade teacher in Des Moines, once wrote a sentence on the blackboard—"The family sat down to dinner"—and asked us to imagine the scene. Then she added a word—"The *Hawaiian* family sat down to dinner"—and asked us to picture the scene again. Everything changed: the room the people were in, what they looked like, the clothes they wore, the food they ate. (This was before the Big Mac and Pizza Hut homogenized the American diet.) By adding only one word, *Hawaiian*, she transformed the whole sentence. I've never forgotten that lesson in what an adjective is and what it can do.

Words that modify—or change—other words are

miraculous inventions. Plain old *family* could mean any family at all. When you modify it with an adjective, in this case *Hawaiian*, you've narrowed the possibilities—ruling out, say, Japanese and Swedish and Nigerian families— but you've also widened the meaning, adding a flavor that wasn't there before. You've made a word, *family*, smaller and larger at the same time. If that's not a miracle, I don't know what is.

Modifiers come in two basic varieties—those that describe things and those that describe actions. What adjectives are to nouns (words for people, places, ideas, and other things), adverbs are to verbs (words for actions).

To appreciate the power of an adverb, imagine a sentence without one: *The family rose from the table.* Then imagine these: *The family rose **sullenly** from the table. The family rose **jubilantly** from the table. The family rose **drunkenly** from the table.* Only one word, *rose*, is modified, yet the entire picture changes.

You can see why modifiers are so popular with writers. Tack on a modifying word or phrase and you get noticeable results with very little work. While you should know how to use modifiers, though, you should also know how not to use them. A skillfully placed modifier can bring a dull sentence back from the dead, but an inept one can be fatal. Think of these tools as weapons: load carefully, conserve ammunition, and always know where they're pointed.

Too Much of a Good Thing

It's no crime to be fond of adjectives and adverbs. Some writers, however, are so enamored that they can't resist slipping in a modifier wherever possible. Every thing and every action—every noun and every verb—is dressed up with a descriptive word or phrase, like cutout clothes on a paper doll. A simple sentence—*Her face glistened in the moonlight*—is not good enough. It has to be dolled up: *Her **tear-stained** face glistened **palely** in the **shimmering** moonlight.*

Adjectives (*tear-stained, shimmering*) and adverbs (*palely*) are meant to make writing colorful and lively. But too many of them can have the opposite effect. Every time you use a modifier, ask yourself whether you need it: Are you telling your readers more? Do they need to know it? Does it do what *Hawaiian* did for *family* or what *sullenly* did for *rose*? Try getting by without the modifier, and if it's not missed, lose it.

Vivid writing doesn't have to be propped up by a lot of modifiers. This sentence from *The Witchfinder*, a mystery by Loren D. Estleman, has almost no modifiers, but it still gives me goose bumps: "In a little while the streetlights would blink on and then the headlamps, a set at a time like bats awakening, and the city would turn itself darkside out like a reversible jacket, shaking out the creatures that breathed and bred in its folds." Think of all the adjectives and adverbs Estleman might have used and wisely didn't.

Statesmen aren't known for rhetorical austerity, but Abraham Lincoln passed up many chances to use modifiers when he wrote the opening of the Gettysburg Address: "Fourscore and seven years ago our fathers brought forth on this continent a new nation conceived in liberty and dedicated to the proposition that all men are created equal."

Of course, he was in a hurry, writing in a train and all,

or so we're told. A writer with more time on his hands might have put it this way: "Fourscore and seven fateful years ago our doughty fathers gamely brought forth on this bonny continent a spunky new nation stoutly conceived in steadfast liberty and pluckily dedicated to the bracing proposition that all men are created utterly equal in perpetuity."

Which version do you like?

The Repeat Offender

Some of us are programmed to dole out modifiers in twos, others in threes, producing prose that has a monotonous regularity. If we're wired for twos, each adjective or adverb is sure to be followed by another. If we're programmed for threes, each modifier is robotically followed by two more.

The result is assembly-line writing: *Lucy's swollen, red cheeks threatened to burst as she stood at the swift, relentless conveyor belt and wildly, desperately stuffed more and more chocolates into her mouth.*

Now let's crank it up a notch: *Lucy's swollen, red, aching cheeks threatened to burst as she stood at the swift, relentless, heartless conveyor belt and wildly, desperately, futilely stuffed more and more and more chocolates into her mouth.*

If you consistently use modifiers in irritating, monotonous, and singsong patterns, break the habit promptly, decisively, and completely.

Rhyme without Reason

Speaking of singsong patterns, here's another—the echo effect. That's what you get when you use a modifier that jingles or rhymes. Think of combinations like *prudent student, delightfully frightful, better sweater, stunningly cunning, ruthlessly truthful, mottled bottle*—don't stop me, I'm on a roll—*abysmally dismal, feral ferret, cruelly grueling, bizarre bazaar, fearful earful, terse nurse.*

Rhyming modifiers come in two varieties: premeditated and unpremeditated. You can easily avoid unpremeditated ones by going over your writing, mentally listening for unintended sound effects. As for the premeditated ones, they aren't necessarily bad. A writer might use an echo effect because it's pleasing (*nicely spiced*), humorous (*doubly bubbly*), or unavoidable (*prime time*). Jingles and rhymes are also used for emphasis or for catchiness in names and titles (*Weed Eater, Roto-Rooter, Famous Amos*). Unfortunately, some combinations that may have been just right the first few times around have grown tattered around the edges: *dream team, true blue, gender bender, white knight, low blow, deep sleep, brain drain, hell's bells.*

Are your ears ringing yet?

The lesson is listen. Think about how your modifiers sound alongside the words they modify. If you don't want to call attention to them, don't make them rhyme or jingle. If you do want to attract attention, be certain it's the right kind. You wouldn't want to use the lighthearted term *legal eagle*, for instance, in a solemn eulogy for a dignified lawyer. Ask yourself: Is this the effect I want? And remember that jingling references to people may have derogatory overtones: *fat cat, plain Jane, shock jock, wise guys, rude dude, wheeler dealer, boy toy.* Those are just the clean ones.

Be sure there's a reason for your rhymes. You'll turn out more inviting writing.

No Assembly Required

One of the big stories of the 1970's, when I was a copy editor for the *Des Moines Register*, was the energy crisis. If people weren't at home fiddling with their thermostats, they were waiting in long lines at the gas station. (Luckily, I drove a Beetle.) Everyone seemed to be talking about OPEC and the geography of the Middle East, home of oil-rich Kuwait. No, not Kuwait—*oil-rich Kuwait*. The name "Kuwait" never appeared alone.

Oil-rich Kuwait introduced me to a literary phenomenon: the prefabricated phrase that appears on cue, saving writers the trouble of coming up with fresh modifiers. These preassembled packages, as I soon learned, are almost everywhere. In a prefab weather report, for example, plain old hail never falls from the sky, only *golf-ball-size* (sometimes *baseball-size*) *hail*.

You've probably read articles that sound like this: **Hastily summoned**, *the world leaders* **seriously considered** *the* **broad initiatives** *and issued a* **measured response** *that promised* **sweeping change** *to deal with the* **overwhelming odds** *that threatened their* **inextricably linked** *economies.*

When descriptive writing is prefabricated, the reader is never surprised. A *question* is *searching*, a *grip* is *viselike*, a *bungalow* is *modest*, *clouds* are *threatening*, a *source* is *reliable*, a *transfusion* is *life-giving*, an *escape* is *narrow*, a *hopeful* is either *young* or *presidential*, *reactions* are *knee-jerk*, and that famous *knoll* is always *grassy*. Still, if you insist on using a prefab expression, at least get it right. I recently saw a real estate ad declaring that a house was "one of its kind." Yes, I'm sure it was.

Modifiers should be fresh, alive, interesting, not predictable. So if a descriptive phrase springs to mind, pre-assembled and ready to use, put it back in the box.

Sort of Disposable

Adjectives and adverbs are supposed to add flavor to your writing, but puny, useless ones only water it down. We toss around these disposable modifiers without really thinking. Come to think of it, *really* is a good example.

It's easy to find throwaways in your writing—just use the Search function in your word processor and look for *very, a little, a bit, pretty, somewhat, sort of, kind of, really, rather,* and *actually.* If a word does nothing but take up space, it's disposable. So dispose of it.

Very, in particular, can become a meaningless tic. Imagine a speech before the Chamber of Commerce: *I'm **very** proud, and **very** honored, to accept this **very** distinguished award on behalf of Mr. Dithers, who is **very** sorry that he could not be here on this **very** special night.*

A latecomer, *overly,* has started showing up in negative sentences. These days, we aren't overly surprised to read sentences like this: *Ariadne's dissertation is not **overly** original.*

I'm not saying that these words are all bad all the time. If what you're after is an informal, chatty tone, perhaps in first-person fiction or a breezy office memo, then *very, a bit, somewhat,* and the rest of the crew might be appropriate. And if you're legitimately using them to make a point, go right ahead. *How late is Ariadne's dissertation? It's **very** late.*

When they're overused, though, such words as *very* are no longer modifiers. They're mere filler, really. (Or do I mean *actually*?)

Misplaced Affections

No matter how we love them, modifiers aren't much good if they're in the wrong place. A word or a phrase may be colorful, even essential, but it can't properly describe something if it's attached to something else.

Here's the kind of unsuitable attachment I mean: *At sixty, those tight swim trunks still make Burt look like a hunk.* The descriptive phrase *at sixty* is supposed to describe Burt, but it's attached to *those tight swim trunks.* Unless the trunks are sixty years old, the modifier is in the wrong place. Put it closer to Burt: *At sixty, Burt still looks like a hunk in those tight swim trunks.* (Okay, Burt, you can breathe now.)

That one was easy. You could have guessed that Burt was sixty, not the swim trunks. But some sentences with badly placed modifiers are harder to figure out: *Tina surprised Harry **wearing her new pumps.***

Who was in the pumps, Tina or Harry? Hey, you never know. Since two people are mentioned before the modifying phrase, *wearing her new pumps,* the reader has to guess who's being described. One possibility: ***Wearing her new pumps**, Tina surprised Harry.* Another: *Tina surprised Harry as he was **wearing her new pumps.***

Most of the time, poorly placed modifiers are harmless. The writer may look silly, but the reader knows what's meant. Only a mind reader could figure this one out: *Paul didn't see Vincent **well***.

Try this: *Vincent wasn't **well** when Paul saw him.* Or: *Paul didn't see **well** when he met Vincent.* For the second meaning, I'd prefer *Paul didn't see Vincent **clearly**.*

Serial Crimes

Imagine you're a food consultant who's been asked to revive a failing restaurant's bill of fare. Your initial proposal might read: *I recommend a radically new menu featuring **pumpkin** ravioli, fettuccine, and linguine.*

Now read the sentence again, and keep your eye on the *pumpkin.* Since it comes at the head of the list, it could refer to all the pasta in the series, not just the ravioli. How fond of pumpkin are you? Do you really want to serve *pumpkin* ravioli, *pumpkin* fettuccine, and *pumpkin* linguine? If so, lots of luck. But if there's supposed to be only one pumpkin dish on the menu, this is a ridiculously easy problem to solve. When an adjective garnishes only one item in a list, put that item last: *I recommend a radically new menu featuring fettuccine, linguine, and **pumpkin** ravioli.*

The same problem can crop up with an adverb in a series. You might write this in a brochure for a health spa: *Our clients **vigorously** exercise, diet, and meditate.* Or: *Our clients diet, meditate, and exercise **vigorously**.* Oh, really? In each case, the modifier, *vigorously*, seems to cover the whole list. Unless these dynamos believe in doing everything vigorously, even meditating, make it: *Our clients diet, meditate, and **vigorously** exercise.*

Putting the modified item last is usually the best solution. With a list of verbs, though, that's not always possible.

Back at the fat farm, suppose you're describing a normal day's routine and you'd like to keep things chronological: *After lunch, clients **lightly** nap, lift weights, and shower.*

Huh? Your patrons probably don't lift weights lightly or shower lightly. But you'd like your list of activities to stay in the same order. In that case, move the adverb (*lightly*) to follow the verb it belongs with (*nap*): *After lunch, clients nap **lightly**, lift weights, and shower.* There's no way a reader would misunderstand that sentence, even skimming lightly.

A phrase that's placed inappropriately in a series can contaminate all the items that follow. Here's a sentence you might find on a Web page for gardeners: *Fungicides are useless against bacteria **that infect plants**, viruses, and insects.*

Exactly how helpless are these fungicides? Are they useless only against bacteria—the kinds that infect plants and viruses and insects? Or are they useless against three different plagues: bacteria, viruses, and insects? If we assume the writer means all three plagues, the solution, again, is to move the confusing phrase, *that infect plants*, to the end of the sentence: *Fungicides are useless against viruses, insects, and bacteria **that infect plants**.*

Superfluous Redundancies

For some writers, once is not enough. They don't beat a dead horse; they beat a *totally* dead horse. They use modifiers that say the same thing as the words they modify. For them, every fact is a *true* fact. They don't expedite; they *speedily* expedite. They don't smell a stench; they smell a *malodorous* stench. In other words, they're redundant. Or as they might put it, *superfluously* redundant.

You might receive a business memo like this from one of these writers:

> *My **final conclusion** is that **preliminary planning** and **exploratory research** by **qualified experts** have **assuredly guaranteed** the **successful triumph** of our **latest new** product. Now that it's **completely finished**, and the **initial debut** is **imminently approaching**, I'm **happily elated** to report that any **perplexing problems** have been **definitively resolved**. Our only competitor of **major significance** is **rigidly inflexible** and **indifferently oblivious** of **market demand**. It's not an **unexpected surprise** that consumers are responding to our **campaign drive** with **positive affirmation**. I suggest that we not only **doggedly persist** in our **prearranged strategy** but also **widely expand** it by offering free gifts.*

Don't you feel like that totally dead horse by now?

When Words Collide

Back in junior high, my friends and I used to trade Tom Swift jokes. The pattern was always the same: a remark by the fictional Tom Swift, followed by the punch line—an adverb. One in particular had me rolling on the floor: *"That's the last time I'll put my arm in a lion's mouth,"* said Tom *offhandedly*. (I was easily amused in those days.)

Tom Swifties were funny because their modifiers could be read two ways, one of them apparently unintentional. The more outrageous they were, the funnier. But if you don't intend to be funny, beware of descriptive words or phrases that could seem ridiculous if taken literally.

Readers will do a double-take if you describe a painting as *priceless* and then give the price it sold for at auction. Likewise, don't say that an invoice is **generally** *specific*, or that a stock fund has **gradually** *skyrocketed*, or that a squabbling committee is **wholly** *divided*. Unless you're making a play on words (*Canapés lead a **hand-to-mouth** existence*), be on the lookout for collisions like these:

*You may leave the table, Dennis, when your plate is **fully** empty.*

*Fashion models are **largely** size four.*

*Dad **clearly** misunderstood.*

*Kirstie finds acupuncture **intensely** relaxing.*

*The gnat is **vastly** minuscule and its brain is **immensely** tiny.*

*Yves likes his coffee **mildly** strong.*

*Little Ricky will grow taller **shortly**.*

*Boris's intentions became **vaguely** clearer.*

*Marcel will **presently** fill us in on the past.*

*The Blandingses bought the house **completely** unfinished.*

*For the Cratchits, poverty was **richly** rewarding.*

*Madalyn **religiously** attended Atheists Anonymous.*

*The computer crash was a **minor** disaster.*

*Miss Pym offered us a slice of **twelve-ounce** pound cake.*

*In October 1929, the market plunged in an **unparalleled** spiral.*

Unless you're curiously indifferent, there's more about illogical writing in chapter 17.

Space Savers

Do you use macros when you work on a computer? They let us store multiple commands on one key, so we can do several things with a single stroke. Sometimes an adjective or adverb acts like a macro. It lets us compress several words of description into one nifty modifier. These sentences, for example, mean the same thing:

*Courtney wore jeans **that were faded** and a shirt **that was dirty** and **full of wrinkles**.*

*Courtney wore **faded** jeans and a **dirty, wrinkled** shirt.*

The second sentence, with its tighter adjectives, makes the first seem loose and flabby. Adverbs can be just as efficient at firming up pudgy sentences. These sentences, which say the same thing, show how one word can do the work of four:

*They dismissed her **in a thoughtless manner**.*

*They dismissed her **thoughtlessly**.*

Of course, you may not always want to cut a description short. If Courtney normally dresses in immaculate Armani suits with nary a thread out of place, you might want to call attention to her dishevelment. Most of the time, though, shorter is better—especially when you're short on room and long on description.

Words in Flight

A little imagination can do a lot more for your descriptive writing than a pageful of adjectives and adverbs. Take a closer look at some of your favorite authors. You'll be surprised at how little their vividness depends on modifiers and how much it owes to imagination.

I'm not necessarily talking about the literary All-Stars. There's imaginative writing in every field, writing that jumps off the page. Whatever your favorite reading is about—birds or cooking or fashion or movies or gardening—that's where you should look for descriptions that aren't smothered in adjectives and adverbs.

Are you a bird-watcher? In one of his field guides, Roger Tory Peterson described the chimney swift as "a cigar with wings" and said the purple finch looked like "a sparrow dipped in raspberry juice." Do you read the fashion pages? Kennedy Fraser, writing about a Balenciaga dress, pictured a woman's legs coming out of the ruffled taffeta "like stamens from a black chrysanthemum."

Gertrude Jekyll, the English landscape architect, wrote that a blanket of columbines looked like "patches in an old, much-washed, cotton patchwork quilt." And the critic Pauline Kael described a noisy, abrasive action movie filmed in the Big Apple as "an aggravated case of New York."

In *The Smithsonian Guides to Natural America*, Suzanne Winckler had this to say of my home state: "Iowa is voluptuous, its landscapes all gentle angles of thighs, elbows, scapulas, vertebrae, and big round buttocks." Wowee!

The food writer M.F.K. Fisher once sneered at party dips as "mixtures to be paddled in by drinkers armed with everything from raw green beans to reinforced potato chips." If that doesn't make you swear off crudités, nothing will. *Good Dog, Bad Dog*, a training book by Mordecai Siegal and Matthew Margolis, compared a seated basset hound to "a jacked-up car with a flat tire."

As I've said before, don't overlook the newspapers. A tribute by Frank DeCaro in the *New York Times* described the late TV talk-show host Virginia Graham's lacquered hairdo as "an abstract form resembling a Dairy Queen soft-serve crossed with the Nike Swoosh."

So the next time an adjective or adverb comes too readily to mind, do what your favorite writers do. Use your imagination instead. Rather than reach for the thesaurus to describe something, imagine it. Think of that little cigar with wings.

12

Too Marvelous for Words

THE SENSIBLE SENTENCE

Like a superhighway, the sentence is a triumph of engineering: the stately capital letter, the procession of words in their proper order, every arch and tunnel, bridge and buttress perfectly fitted to its job.

If many writers believe bigger is better, who can blame them? Building a sentence can give you a thrill. It's easy to become infatuated with your own words, and once you get started you hate to stop. The noble pageant goes on and on, especially if you've discovered dashes and semicolons, and gluey words like *however* and *nevertheless*. Your mighty sentence swells, as does your head. "Awesome," you think.

Your poor readers, meanwhile, trudge on, peering wistfully toward the horizon in search of a period. They soon lose track of the subject, and the mighty sentence becomes a road to nowhere.

What went wrong? Length alone isn't the answer. If you've been told that short sentences are always better than long ones, forget it. It's better to mix them up, because writing that has too many short, choppy sentences is just as tedious as writing that has too many long ones. What matters most with any sentence, short or long, is how it's put together. A long sentence will hold up if it's structurally sound, and a short one will collapse if it's not properly constructed.

This business about sentence construction isn't some abstract idea. It can determine whether your writing makes sense. Let's inspect some of the structural flaws that can undermine sentences.

Speed Bumps

When a sentence works, we can follow it smoothly from beginning to end. If you saw this one in your local paper, you'd have to read it twice:

> *The get-rich-quick scheme that Karl LaFong, the former mayor, and Egbert Souse and Cuthbert J. Twillie, his confederates, cooked up—a theme park built on alligator-infested swampland near a derelict nuclear power plant on the northern outskirts of the city—is believed to have bankrupted some of Lakeville's leading citizens.*

The problem with the sentence isn't its length but its bumpy construction. Ideas don't follow one another smoothly. One interrupts another (bump!), and is interrupted in turn (bump!), until we lose the point of the sentence.

Look again at some of the speed bumps. The subject in the sentence is that *get-rich-quick scheme*. But before we learn what mayhem the scheme caused (the point of the sentence), we hit two teeth-rattling bumps, interrupting to tell us (1) who did the fleecing and (2) what the scam was about. Even those interruptions get interrupted. No wonder we lose our way.

Here's a version that gives us one idea at a time:

> *Former Mayor Karl LaFong and his confederates Egbert Souse and Cuthbert J. Twillie are believed to have bankrupted some of Lakeville's leading citizens with a get-rich-quick scheme—a theme park built on alligator-infested swampland near a derelict nuclear power plant on the northern outskirts of the city.*

It's still a whopping big sentence, bigger than I'd like, but it works. It gives the reader one idea at a time, each completed before another is introduced. No speed bumps, thank you.

Long Division

In the hands of our best writers, long sentences can knock your socks off. In this passage from *Rabbit, Run*, John Updike alternates long and short sentences to build suspense as Rabbit Angstrom, cigarette in mouth, shoots a basket before a group of schoolboys.

"As they stare hushed he sights squinting through blue clouds of weed smoke, a suddenly dark silhouette like a smokestack against the afternoon spring sky, setting his feet with care, wiggling the ball with nervousness in front of his chest, one widespread white hand on top of the ball and the other underneath, jiggling it patiently to get some adjustment in air itself. The cuticle moons on his finger-nails are big. Then the ball seems to ride up the right lapel of his coat and comes off his shoulder as his knees dip down, and it appears the ball will miss because though he shot from an angle the ball is not going toward the back-board. It was not aimed there. It drops into the circle of the rim, whipping the net with a ladylike whisper."

We can follow a long sentence when it's presented one idea at a time. But often, long sentences are too much to swallow. This one would choke a horse:

> *The play of moonlight and shadow in the darkened, unfamiliar kitchen, which reminded Fergie of her boarding school days and her daring midnight raids on the pantry, hair-raising adventures that could have gotten her expelled, made it difficult for her to copy her mother-in-law's secret recipe for Windsor compote.*

Unless a long sentence demands to be consumed in one gulp, break it in two:

> *The play of moonlight and shadow in the darkened, unfamiliar kitchen made it difficult for Fergie to copy her mother-in-law's recipe for Windsor compote. She was reminded of her boarding school days and those daring midnight raids on the pantry, hair-raising adventures that could have gotten her expelled.*

Don't rule out long sentences—just remember that they're hard to write well. If you've written a long sentence and you're not sure that it works, it probably doesn't.

Break it up. Not many writers can handle long sentences as gracefully as Updike.

Betwixt and Between

There's an old saying that it's not the pearls that make a necklace—it's the string. The parts of a sentence won't make a necklace, either, without something to hold them together.

This sentence, for example, has no string: *Warren says the stock is undervalued, he doesn't know whether it's hit bottom yet.*

It sounds as if there's something missing, doesn't it? That's because the example isn't really a sentence. It's two sentences trying to be one. This sin of omission is sometimes called a run-on sentence because, well, it runs on. Its parts are unconnected, like pearls without a string. The comma alone can't hold them together.

There are three ways to fix a sentence whose parts aren't joined correctly:

- Add a connecting word (*and, but, or, although, however,* etc.): *Warren says the stock is undervalued,* **but** *he doesn't know whether it's hit bottom yet.*
- Use a semicolon instead of a comma: *Warren says the stock is undervalued; he doesn't know whether it's hit bottom yet.*
- Break the sentence in two: *Warren says the stock is undervalued. He doesn't know whether it's hit bottom yet.*

All three are correct. But since the two-sentence version is choppy and the semicolon seems too formal, my choice in this case is to add a connecting word.

Be careful about some connecting words, however. In fact, let's use *however* as an example. It's often misused because writers don't make clear which part of the sentence it goes with: *Warren says the stock is undervalued,* **however,** *he doesn't know whether it's hit bottom yet.*

Where does *however* belong, with the first part of the sentence or the second? Here's how to fix a *however* problem:

- Make two sentences, attaching *however* to the appropriate one. You could mean this: *Warren says the stock is undervalued,* **however.** *He doesn't know whether it's hit bottom yet.* Or perhaps this: *Warren says the stock is undervalued.* **However,** *he doesn't know whether it's hit bottom yet.*
- Use a semicolon and attach *however* to the appropriate part of the sentence. You might mean this: *Warren says the stock is undervalued,* **however;** *he doesn't know whether it's hit bottom yet.* Or this: *Warren says the stock is undervalued;* **however,** *he doesn't know whether it's hit bottom yet.*

Before sharing your pearls of wisdom, make sure there are strings attached.

13

Made for Each Other

WELL-MATCHED SENTENCES

Gosh, I admire hosts who seat dinner guests perfectly every time, who have a knack for arranging a group of strangers so the conversation never flags. Seated differently, these same guests might endure an evening of awkward, throat-clearing silences.

I also admire people who know instinctively how to arrange sentences. Every sentence is in the right place and leads comfortably to the next. Ideas fall naturally into line. For some writers, putting sentences together naturally is a gift. The rest of us have to learn how to make our sentences compatible. Happily, it's not hard to help them mingle.

The Lineup

When you feel your writing is choppy and disjointed—or when someone else tells you it is—suspect that a sentence is out of line. If a reader has to rearrange sentences to follow your thinking, then the sentences are in the wrong order.

You might find an example like this in the business pages of your newspaper, especially if the copy editors are on vacation:

Nervous investors struggled all day to understand the significance of the sell-off. Just before the market closed, a spokesman for Netscape said the company had no comment. The Dow's steep plunge followed early-morning rumors that Netscape would buy Microsoft.

The sentences seem disjointed because the thoughts are out of order. Readers can't appreciate the significance of the first two sentences (investor nervousness and Netscape's no comment) until they find out what everyone was so upset about (the Dow's steep plunge and the takeover rumors). Notice how everything falls into place when we put the last sentence at the head of the lineup:

The Dow's steep plunge followed early-morning rumors that Netscape would buy Microsoft. Nervous investors struggled all day to understand the significance of the sell-off. Just before the market closed, a spokesman for Netscape said the company had no comment.

The sentences now mingle naturally because they follow one another logically.

A zealous library volunteer might have written this

notice for the community newsletter. What do you make of the lineup?

Books can't circulate when they're on your shelves instead of ours. So please return any overdue books you have at home. Overdue books are a serious problem for our library. If you don't bring them back, we'll post your name on the bulletin board.

Now, that's not a terrible piece of writing. All the necessary information is there, and each sentence reads well. But something feels wrong. Look at the order of the sentences. One of them—*Overdue books are a serious problem for our library*—interrupts two others that are clearly a couple and shouldn't be separated. Where does the stray belong? I'd put it up front, where the train of thought begins, since it tells us why the notice is being written in the first place:

Overdue books are a serious problem for our library. Books can't circulate when they're on your shelves instead of ours. So please return any overdue books you have at home. If you don't bring them back, we'll post your name on the bulletin board.

Your sentences will be easier to follow if they're in logical order. Unless you have some reason to do otherwise— you're building suspense, perhaps, or saving a surprise for last—keep them orderly. Search for stray sentences, then put them where they belong.

Getting to Know You

If your sentences are in the right order but still seem disjointed, maybe they haven't been properly introduced.

One way to introduce them is to ask yourself what they have in common, then move their common interests closer together.

You might find a passage like this in a paper for a science class:

> *Edison worked as a telegraph operator for the Grand Trunk Railroad after dropping out of school. When he produced his first inventions, among them a means of sending multiple messages simultaneously, this experience came in handy.*

The sentences themselves aren't bad. Each one reads well, and they're plainly in the right order. But as a couple, they seem a bit stiff and uncomfortable. To strengthen their bond, bring their common interest—Edison's telegraph experience—closer together:

> *After dropping out of school, **Edison worked as a telegraph operator for the Grand Trunk Railroad.** **This experience** came in handy when he produced his first inventions, among them a means of sending multiple messages simultaneously.*

Sentences are more comfortable together when the things they have in common are closer. Here are two more sentences that should get to know each other better:

> *Before the FDIC began insuring deposits in 1933, many people lost their life savings in bank failures. After the banking regulations were enacted, such losses became rare.*

These sentences have two ideas in common: banking laws and lost savings. One way to get them better acquainted is to move the two sections on bank regulations closer together:

Many people lost their life savings in bank failures
before **the FDIC began insuring deposits in 1933.**
After the banking regulations were enacted, *such*
losses became rare.

Another way is to move the two sections on lost savings closer together:

Before the FDIC began insuring deposits in 1933,
many people lost their life savings in bank failures.
Such losses became rare *after the banking regulations were enacted.*

Which way is better? That depends on which idea is more important to you. The first solution emphasizes the losses; the second, the banking regulations. Either way, the sentences work better when they have a common touch.

The Right Connections

I'm an incorrigible matchmaker. If I think two people are made for each other, I can't resist trying to bring them together. Sometimes we have to be matchmakers when we write, too. Sentences that are meant for each other may need a little help from their friends.

If sentences don't click, even though they're in the right order and have interests in common, they need something else to unite them. What's missing may be a connecting word or phrase to help the reader see why one sentence should follow the other.

These connections include *also, and, as, at any rate, because, besides, but, furthermore, however, in the meantime, nevertheless, on the other hand, or, so, then, therefore, thus,* and *yet.* (If you've been taught that it's incorrect to begin a sentence with *and* or *but,* you've been taught incorrectly.

Look it up: Conjunctions are for joining words, phrases, clauses, *and* sentences.)

The right connection between sentences explains their relationship. It tells us why they belong where they are. Perhaps one sentence adds an idea to another, or clarifies an idea already mentioned. Maybe it zooms in for a close-up, or maybe it zooms out for the big picture. Maybe a sentence tells us the cause or the result of something that happened in another.

Whatever the relationship, it has to be obvious. When one sentence doesn't smoothly follow another, the reader feels disconnected. If you read this in a college newspaper, for example, you might not get the connection:

> *The food manager has been inundated by com-*
> *plaints since the dining hall stopped serving three-*
> *alarm-chili dogs. They'll soon be back on the menu.*
> *The price will go up 50 cents.*

The sentences are in the right order and have interests in common, but there's still some distance between them. We need connecting words to alert the reader that the second sentence is a result of the first, and that the third one puts a damper on the second:

> *The food manager has been inundated by com-*
> *plaints since the dining hall stopped serving three-*
> *alarm-chili dogs. **As a consequence**, they'll soon be*
> *back on the menu. **However**, the price will go up*
> *50 cents. (A more casual writer might say: **So** they'll*
> *soon be back on the menu. **But** the price will go up*
> *50 cents.)*

Those sentences aren't just touching. They're holding hands.

14

Give Me a Break

THINKING IN PARAGRAPHS

Jazz aficionados will know this story. The great saxophonist John Coltrane was troubled because his solos were running way too long. He couldn't figure out how to end his improvisations. His friend Miles Davis had a suggestion. "John," he said, "put the horn down."

Some writers have the same problem. They have a propensity for immensity. Their paragraphs run way too long, and they can't seem to find the end. They'd do well to follow Miles's advice. Put the horn down. Hit the paragraph key.

Don't misunderstand me. I'm not saying long paragraphs don't belong in good writing. When they work, they're not too long—they're just long enough. (I'm a Proust fan myself.) But as a rule, short paragraphs are easier to write, easier to read, easier to understand.

I think I hear a dissenting voice: "What's wrong with long paragraphs? You see them everywhere—just pick up an academic journal and turn to any page. Long paragraphs are evidence of the higher mind at work."

Sometimes they are. But sometimes they're evidence of a confused mind or a disorganized mind or a mind that's trying to impress.

The length of a paragraph isn't a measure of its intellectual depth. A paragraph expresses a train of thought, and some trains are longer than others. When one gets too long, it should probably be two. If the engine is too far from the caboose, it's hauling too much freight.

You may object that your train of thought is a very long one. But that doesn't mean it's indivisible. I'll bet there's a pause somewhere along the way, a slight shift in focus, a mental intake of breath. Hit the paragraph key! If you need to take a breath, so does the reader.

The reader, after all, is why paragraphs were invented. A solid, unbroken blob of type—whether on a page or on a screen—doesn't invite us to read or make us want to keep reading. We need a break every now and then, a chance to digest one thought before going on to another.

A Sight for Sore Eyes

Our eyes can use an occasional break, too, you know. If you were to read this paragraph in a consultant's report, your eyes would glaze over:

The city of Freedonia must be prepared for development on all land that is vacant or underdeveloped—about twelve percent of the total acreage. To estimate the development potential of these parcels, our chief planner, Professor Quincy Adams Wagstaff, weighed the physical, regulatory, and environmental constraints. Taking these into consideration, he estimates that about half of this land is developable, excluding easements for the viaduct. Development pressures will continue to increase while Sylvania, Dukesbury, and other neighboring municipalities become more developed and people are attracted by the character of your city. As our legal adviser, J. Cheever Loophole, has pointed out, the challenge is not whether to grow, because growth is inevitable. The challenge is to find a way to grow while preserving the ambience of Freedonia.

Quite an eyeful, isn't it? You might argue that the paragraph is reasonable as it is. You might even like it, since it does seem to follow one train of thought from beginning to end. Well, I like cheeseburgers but I don't try to swallow them whole. I'd recommend breaking the paragraph in two after the word *viaduct*. Why *viaduct*? Because a shift in focus takes place there, as the writer turns from statistics to what it all means. Now read the example again, this time as two paragraphs. It's no less reasonable, and the reader gets a break.

The city of Freedonia must be prepared for development on all land that is vacant or underdeveloped—about twelve percent of the total acreage. To estimate

*the development potential of these parcels, our chief
planner, Professor Quincy Adams Wagstaff, weighed
the physical, regulatory, and environmental constraints. Taking these into consideration, he estimates
that about half of this land is developable, excluding
easements for the viaduct.*

*Development pressures will continue to increase
while Sylvania, Dukesbury, and other neighboring
municipalities become more developed and people
are attracted by the character of your city. As our
legal adviser, J. Cheever Loophole, has pointed out,
the challenge is not whether to grow, because growth
is inevitable. The challenge is to find a way to grow
while preserving the ambience of Freedonia.*

Pauses aren't merely restful. They're convenient in
other ways as well. By dividing a piece of writing into eye-
size chunks, paragraphs help readers who want to review
what they've read. I find paragraphs especially useful
when I want to reread a passage, refresh my memory
quickly, or find my place again after stopping to check on
the soufflé or walk the Rottweilers.

If all a paragraph did was give the reader a break, that
would be enough. But it does something even more important. Each pause is a signal from the writer that one
train of thought has passed and another is arriving.

That's why you can't just start a new paragraph every
two sentences, say, or every three or four. A new one
should begin when a new idea comes along. By "new idea"
I don't mean a complete change of topic. If a paragraph
gets too long, you might divide it where there's a shift in
the direction, the perspective, or the focus (as in the Free-

donia example, when we moved from the details to the big picture). Or if there's an important sentence buried deep inside, you might use it to start a new paragraph.

No matter what they say, size does matter.

Nice Work If You Can Get It

Each sentence in a paragraph has a job—to nudge the main idea along. If a sentence isn't doing its job, it doesn't belong in the paragraph. I know it's hard to dump a nifty sentence you like simply because it doesn't fit in. But a writer's got to do what a writer's got to do.

Let's take a look at a few sentences that might have been written for an ornithological journal:

> *The courtship behavior of the reclusive bristle-rumped partridge is unique and rarely observed. Native only to Utah, the partridge performs its mating dance entirely on one leg, the male on the right leg and the hen on the left. As with other grouse, the male is polygamous. One mating pair, recorded by Dr. Rufous Piper, performed the ceremonial dance while hopping in concentric circles, grooming each other's bristles and waving their free legs in the air.*

With one exception, each sentence advances the paragraph's main subject, the birds' unique mating ritual. Yes, as you've probably guessed, the sentence about the male's polygamy belongs in some other paragraph. The polygamy isn't unique, and it has nothing to do with the mating dance.

A Sense of Purpose

Just as each sentence in a paragraph has a job, so does each paragraph. Sentences advance the main idea of a paragraph, and paragraphs advance the main idea—the purpose—of the piece you're writing. In both cases, you're using a part to move the reader farther along in the whole.

The difference, though, is that paragraphs aren't knit as closely together as sentences. The leap from paragraph to paragraph is bigger than the leap from sentence to sentence. That's because successive paragraphs don't necessarily get us from here to there by moving in a straight line. They can change direction by giving us something new. They can change focus by moving from the specific to the general or vice versa. Or they can change perspective by showing us a subject from a different angle.

Like sentences, paragraphs can be in the right order and still not follow one another smoothly. You may need a bridge to link them, to let the reader know where you're going. That's why we have such expressions as *on the other hand* and *to make matters worse* and *meanwhile*.

Keep in mind that change is what a new paragraph is all about, and readers know that. Paragraphs don't have to hold hands the way sentences do. It's enough that they share a sense of purpose.

The Elongated Yellow Fruit

FEAR OF REPETITION

Some writers think there's an unwritten rule against repeating themselves. They'll do anything to avoid using the same word twice in the same passage, coming up with ungainly synonyms only the late Mr. Roget could love.

Put down the thesaurus. A snake by any other name wouldn't be as snakelike. Why call it a serpent the second time it slithers into view, a legless reptile the next time, and a member of the suborder Ophidia the time after that? Editors call this phobia "elegant variation." Charles W. Morton called it the "elongated-yellow-fruit school of writing," for people who can't bring themselves to use "banana" twice. A word that's just right is always better than a lame imitation.

Fear of repetition is especially common among journalists. In the belief that variety is creativity, many of them go through painful contortions to avoid using an important word twice:

> *As the Cardinal briefed the Pope on plans for the*
> *Holy Father's visit, His Eminence told His Holiness*
> *that the Pontiff's trip was eagerly awaited by wor-*
> *shipers who had never seen God's Vicar in person.*

If you're guilty of writing like that, cease and desist. Skilled writers (some are even journalists) know they can use repetition to their advantage, building power with each echo of a word or phrase or sound. You're already familiar with some famous examples, from Shakespeare ("And Brutus is an honorable man") to Lincoln ("of the people, by the people, for the people") to James Joyce ("and yes I said yes I will Yes") to the Reverend Martin Luther King, Jr. ("I have a dream"). Thank heavens they didn't avoid repeating themselves. What if Poe's Raven had squawked "Nevermore" only once and never more? I cringe to imagine it: *Quoth the Raven, "Fat chance,"* or *"In a pig's eye,"* or *"Not bloody likely."*

Variety is a wonderful thing, and I'm not putting it down. But when carried to ridiculous extremes, it has a monotony of its own.

Nicely Nicely

The same can be said of repetition, of course. There are times when enough is enough is enough. Gertrude Stein, who nearly made a fetish of repetition, has been both ridiculed and acclaimed for it. You can decide for yourself. Here's a typical passage of hers:

"He had been nicely faithful. In being one he was one who had he been one continuing would not have been one continuing being nicely faithful. He was one continuing, he was not continuing to be nicely faithful. In continuing he was being one being the one who was saying good good, excellent but in continuing he was needing that he was believing that he was aspiring to be one continuing to be able to be saying good good, excellent."

One editor turned down a manuscript of Stein's with this explanation: "Being only one, having only one pair of eyes, having only one time, having only one life, I cannot read your MS three or four times. Not even one time. Only one look, only one look is enough. Hardly one copy would sell here. Hardly one. Hardly one."

16

Training Wheels

BELABORING
THE OBVIOUS

Remember when you needed training wheels to ride a bike? Well, some grown-ups still use them—when they write. They shore up their prose, belaboring the obvious with unnecessary words.

When you write with props, you don't say merely that a melody is pleasing, you say that it's pleasing *to the ear*. A dancer isn't just graceful, she's graceful *on her feet*. Take off the training wheels. You don't need them and neither do your readers.

You'll have to search carefully for props in your writing because they're hidden in plain sight. The obvious, as we all know, can be hard to see.

Look first at phrases starting with prepositions (*by, for, in, of, on, to,* and so on), and be sure they're necessary. This sentence includes a classic example of an unnecessary prop: *Tom planned **in advance** to steal the jam.* Since planning is generally done ahead of time, who needs *in advance?*

People toss off redundant expressions when their minds are elsewhere. Pretty soon they don't notice them. Someone fond of prop words might write a real estate flyer that reads like this:

*The Neo-Tuscan farmhouse is filled **to the rafters** with charm. Barn-red **in color**, it is built of hand-made Belgian brick that was flown in **by plane** from Bruges. Situated on a rise **of ground** amid formal gardens, the house is minimalist **in design** yet spacious **in size**. It's an easy drive **by car** to prime shopping, and a leisurely walk **on foot** to a secluded nature preserve.*

A prepositional phrase that doesn't add anything should be subtracted. If you're unsure, just imagine that the phrase isn't there. Then, if it isn't missed, drop it. Don't put up with things that are *sour **to the taste**, soft **to the touch**,* haughty **in manner**, *stocky **in build**,* ringed **around the edge**, *rough **in texture**,* short **in stature**, *pretty **in appearance**, assembled **in a group**, sturdy **in construction**,* or *given away **for nothing**.*

Another kind of prop is the unnecessary adjective or adverb (these are words describing things or actions). Reconsider such expressions as ***piercing** scream,* ***sudden** start,* ***advance** reservations,* ***future** plans,* ***forward** progress,* ***initial** beginning,* and that old ***upward** surge.* And try to avoid *demanding **insistently**, screeching **loudly**, seeing **visually**,* *experiencing **personally**, concealing **secretively**,* and *filing* **singly** onto a bus. There's more about this problem in chapter 11.

Pay attention. Prop words sneak into your writing when your mind is elsewhere. I've used them myself, but that's past history.

17

Critique of Poor Reason

THE ART OF
MAKING SENSE

Your first duty to the reader is to make sense. Everything else—eloquence, beautiful images, catchy phrases, melodic and rhythmic language—comes later, if at all. I'm all for artistry, but it's better to write something homely and clear than something lovely and unintelligible.

Of course, no one sets out to write nonsense. We do it because we're careless with words. We know what we mean, naturally, but others can't read our minds. Words are all a reader has. What makes perfect sense to us might seem illogical, incoherent, insensitive, or silly to someone else.

Say you're recommending a new kind of software to your boss. Don't say it's *incomparable*, then go on to compare it to Microsoft's version. Don't call two things *virtually identical*, then list their many differences. Too often we write on automatic pilot, not giving enough thought to the meaning of our words.

Thoughtless writing might even be unintentionally cruel. A talented city official who happens to be a double amputee might be offended if you called him the mayor's *right-hand man*. Then again, he might not. In some circumstances, ordinary expressions can be hurtful or inappropriate. A casual phrase that's acceptable in conversation (saying that a blind person has failed to *see* a point, for example, or that a deaf person didn't *listen*) might look insensitive on the page. If in doubt, take it out.

Fools Rush In

The best way to avoid using a word or phrase foolishly is to think about all of its possible meanings. Take the word *penniless*. We all know what it means: *poor*. But what if Bill Cosby takes a handful of change out of his pocket and discovers he doesn't have any pennies? To call him *penniless* would be accurate, strictly speaking. But it would be a dumb thing to write unless you were trying to be funny.

Everyone who writes has common sense to some degree. But we don't all use it as often as we should. We become careless about what we've written, never imagining it might look silly to readers. If you don't want them to snicker, don't write sentences like these:

Milton found that he was lost.

Françoise struck a candid pose.

Olga bent over backward to please her gymnastics coach.

Martha says tortilla chips are handy in a crunch.

There was a stony silence at the granite quarry.

The search for Santa Fe's first street turned up an alley.

A ton of cocaine is nothing to sneeze at.

You might say those examples fill a much-needed gap.

The Overactive Imagination

An imaginative flourish here or there can make dry writing come to life. But ill-considered imagery can create the wrong picture—or too many pictures. Put yourself in the reader's place and think about the images you've created. They might be unintentionally ditsy, as in these examples:

Mrs. Proudie left no stone unturned in her search for a son-in-law. Maybe her daughter goes for worms.

As Jethro ate squid for the first time, his heart was in his throat. Heimlich maneuver, anyone?

Some writers think two images are twice as nice, but they're only half right. Two is a crowd, especially if they're within spitting distance of each other, as they are here:

Tonya's ace in the hole took the wind out of Nancy's sails.

Mario was on a wild-goose chase and ran out of steam.

When Job got the short end of the stick, it was the last straw.

A dyed-in-the-wool vegan doesn't cotton to meatballs.

Daisy and Tom didn't see eye to eye, so she gave him an earful.

Don't make too many demands on the reader's imagination. One image at a time, please.

References Required

Our writing would be awfully klutzy if we had to repeat ourselves whenever we referred to something already mentioned. Luckily, we don't have to. There are proxies we can substitute for words or phrases we've used before. But a proxy—especially *this, that, which, here, there, now, then*—can be misleading if it's used thoughtlessly. The problem comes up when we've mentioned more than one thing and the reader has to guess which one the proxy refers to.

A research paper on dietary habits in small countries might include this sentence: *Every day the average adult in Grand Fenwick consumes two gallons of raw milk, **which** can be dangerous.*

What's dangerous? The raw milk? Or drinking gallons at a time? The writer probably means the milk, so here's a solution: *The average adult in Grand Fenwick consumes raw milk, **which** can be dangerous, at the rate of two gallons a day.* That's awkward, perhaps, but it's clear. I'd rather drop *which* entirely: *Raw milk can be dangerous, but the average adult in Grand Fenwick consumes two gallons a day.*

Sometimes *that* is the question. Imagine this sentence in a customer's complaint to a bookshop: *You claim the book is rare because it's a first edition, but **that**'s incorrect.*

What's incorrect? That the book is rare? Or that it's a first edition? There are several possibilities. The customer could mean this: *You claim the book is rare, but **that**'s incorrect, even though it is a first edition.* Or perhaps this: *You claim the book is a first edition, but **that**'s incorrect, even though it is rare.* I'd find it more graceful to drop *that*. For example, *The book is a first edition, as you claim, but it's not rare.*

In the next sentence, which we might see in an Internet newsgroup, there's more than one *there* there: *I said the software was compatible so the hard drive wouldn't crash, but I was mistaken **there**.*

Exactly where is *there*? Was the writer mistaken about the software, the hard drive, or both? Assuming the worst, make it: *I said the software was compatible, but I was mistaken **there**, so the hard drive crashed.*

Computers can get us into trouble in more ways than one. You might find this item on a hackers' bulletin board: *Kevin couldn't stop breaking into the Pentagon computer system even though the FBI was watching him, **now** that he was an Internet celebrity.*

What does the sentence mean? Now that Kevin's a celebrity, he can't stop? Or now that he's a celebrity, the FBI is watching? Here's one solution: ***Now** that he was an Internet celebrity, Kevin couldn't stop breaking into the Pentagon computer system, even though the FBI was watching him.*

People don't normally read a sentence in a vacuum. They can usually figure out what it means. But they shouldn't have to. If there's any chance that readers might misunderstand, tinker with the sentence.

Say It Isn't So

An explanation can be confusing when it tells us why something isn't so. The danger signs are the words *not* and *because*. Used together, they can tangle an explanation in *not*s.

Can you untie this one? *He did not marry her because she was a Methodist.* Do you see why that sentence is tangled? No, it has nothing to do with religion or romance.

The problem is that the sentence can be read in two ways. It could mean: *Because she was a Methodist, he did not marry her.* Or: *He married her, but not because she was a Methodist.* We shouldn't have to be mind readers to understand an explanation.

The *not* is just as slippery if it's part of a contraction. Try to find the two possible explanations here: *A.J. didn't change the tires because he was doing practice laps the next day.*

Did he or didn't he change the tires? Make it: *Because he was doing practice laps the next day, A.J. didn't change the tires.* Or: *A.J. changed the tires, but not because he was doing practice laps the next day.*

Why worry about a few *not*s? Because making sense is the most important part of writing. That makes sense, doesn't it?

Grammar Moses

THOU SHALT NOT EMBARRASS THYSELF

You think nobody cares about grammar? The next time you post a message to an Internet newsgroup, try mixing up *it's* and *its, lie* and *lay,* or *there* and *their,* and see what happens. The grammar police will be on your case, and you'll get so many flames that your modem will smoke.

Believe me, people care. Whether you're writing e-mail or snail mail, a Web page or a page of a memoir, grammar counts. Readers may dismiss writing that's otherwise okay, even terrific, if the grammar is screwed up. This is no small matter, particularly when you're trying to make a good impression—applying for a job, say, or trying to sell a book proposal, or writing an essay for admission to college.

It's a good bet, though, that your grammar isn't perfect. If you didn't learn it in school (like most Americans under forty) or if you've forgotten what you were taught, buy a grammar book and keep it right beside your dictionary. Don't be intimidated. Grammar books aren't as forbidding and textbooky as they used to be, and not all of them bristle with technical terms. You don't need to know the heavy terminology, anyway. You can be a good driver even if you can't name all the parts of a car.

This chapter is no substitute for a grammar book. But until you get one, here's a look at some of the blunders that writers make most often.

An I for an I

Hugh Downs, who often wraps up *20/20* broadcasts by saying, "Good night from Barbara and me," has gotten indignant letters from viewers who think, mistakenly, that he should be saying "from Barbara and I." I hear that the same thing used to happen to Harry Reasoner when he did the evening news with Barbara Walters.

Perhaps the single most common mistake in grammar these days is using *I* instead of *me*. "This is just between you and *I*," a friend writes conspiratorially. Or a colleague says in a memo, "The boss humiliated Ellen and *I*." Or Aunt Agatha writes, "Happy Birthday from Uncle Miltie and *I*."

It's *me*, it's *me*, it's *me*, O Lord!

So what's *I* got that *me* doesn't? Many people seem to feel that *I* is somehow classier than *me*, probably because of all the nagging they got as kids for saying, "Me want Twinkies," or "Me hate broccoli." They're left with the impression that there's something second-rate about *me*. Impressions like that are hard to overcome, but a trick might help.

When *I* or *me* appears by itself, we never mess up. No one says, "The boss humiliated *I*." So when *I* or *me* is part of a pair, just eliminate the other guy. In Aunt Agatha's note, for example, get rid of Uncle Miltie: *Happy Birthday from me*; then put him back in the picture: *Happy Birthday from Uncle Miltie and me*. Give it a try.

The same trick works with *he* and *him*, *she* and *her*, *they* and *them*, and other pronouns (words that stand in for nouns, like *Ike*, *Lassie*, or *the Nelsons*). Take the sentence *Ricky saw **she** and David at the mall*. Is it *she* or *her*? Lose David and the answer is obvious: *Ricky saw **her** [and David] at the mall*.

Remember, too, that a pronoun at the front of a sentence is more likely to be a subject (*I, he, she, they,* etc.), while one at the back is more likely to be an object (*me, him, her, them*). When you have to guess, play the odds.

The Agreeable Writer

"I don't want to talk grammar, I want to talk like a lady," said Eliza Doolittle, the flower peddler in George Bernard Shaw's *Pygmalion*. Sorry, but we can't talk or write well without using words correctly. So let's talk grammar some more.

A big part of grammar is matching up the verb (the action word) with the subject (who or what is doing the action). If a subject is singular, the verb is too. If the actor is plural, so is the action word. Nobody should have trouble with a simple sentence, such as *Linda tapes every phone call.* The subject, *Linda,* is singular and so is the verb, *tapes.* But what if the sentence isn't so simple? Let's toss in something extra between the subject and the verb: *Linda, along with her techie friends, [tape or tapes] every phone call.* Which is it? No, the verb doesn't change. Since *Linda* is still the subject, the verb is still singular: *tapes.*

When you come across a sentence with a lot of information separating the subject and the verb, don't be misled. Phrases such as *along with, as well as, together with,* and *in addition to* don't change a singular subject. Mentally eliminate the extra stuff and you won't go wrong.

The Terrible Twos

Familiarity breeds contemptible grammar. Some words are misused so often that the errors start to look right. How many times have you read something like, *Sleeping Beauty **laid** down for a nap,* or *Bill should train Buddy not to **lay** in the driveway*? Close, but no cigar. Sleeping Beauty *lay* down, and Buddy should be taught where to *lie.*

Many English words are easy to confuse because they look and sound so much alike. *Lie* and *lay* are good examples, along with *their* and *there, its* and *it's,* and *your* and *you're.* Here are some quick reminders to make sure you use them correctly.

- *Lie* and *lay.* To *lie* is to recline: *Camille often **lies** on the divan. Last night she **lay** on the divan. For days she **has lain** on the divan.* To *lay* is to place: *Sluggo **lays** his heart at Nancy's feet. On Sunday he **laid** his heart at her feet. Every night he **has laid** his heart at* *her feet.* A memory aid: Notice how you can hear the word *lie* in *recline,* and *lay* in *place.*

- *Their* **and** *there.* Remember them this way. *Their* is a possessive (a word that shows ownership) and has the word *heir* in it: **Their** *heir inherited* **their** *hair.* As for *there,* it refers to a place; it's like *here* and has *here* in it: *He blew his inheritance here and* **there.**
- *Its* **and** *it's.* This one is easy. *Its* is possessive, and *it's* is short for *it is* or *it has.* (In contractions, such as *it's,* apostrophes stand for missing letters.) So if you can substitute *it is* or *it has,* use *it's. When the parakeet is cranky,* **its** *squawk means* **it's** *hungry.*
- *Your* **and** *you're.* Same principle. If you can substitute *you are,* go for *you're.* **Your** *attitude proves* **you're** *a ninny.*

You'll save yourself plenty of grief if you remember that pronouns don't have apostrophes when they're possessive (*hers, his, its, ours, their, theirs, your, yours*). They have apostrophes only in contractions; the apostrophes stand for missing letters: *I'm* (for *I am*), *we've* (*we have*), *she'd* (*she would*), *they're* (*they are*), and so on. Engrave it on your brain.

Taking Leave of Your Tenses

Tenses are the time zones of writing, and you can't be in two zones at the same time. Even the Concorde can't be in Pacific and Mountain times at once. When writers are careless with tenses, readers get lost along the way.

Tenses let readers know when something happened, is happening, or will happen. We can say: *Today Ralph drives a bus. Yesterday Ralph drove a bus. The day before, Ralph had driven a bus. Tomorrow Ralph will drive a bus. By next fall Ralph will have driven a bus for twenty years.* Simple enough. We're just telling time with verbs.

But when there's more going on in a sentence—it has two verbs, maybe three—the tenses have to make sense together.

A supervisor in a hurry might write this recommendation: *When duty calls, Ralph answered.* That sentence has a foot in one time zone and a foot in another. Duty's call and Ralph's answer should happen at roughly the same time. But in the example, duty *calls* in the present while Ralph *answered* in the past.

When things happen at the same time, the tenses of the verbs have to be the same: *When duty **calls**, Ralph **answers**.* Or: *When duty **called**, Ralph **answered**.*

The goings-on in a sentence don't always go on at the same time, however: *Ralph **says** he **drove** yesterday and **will drive** next week.* When we write about things that happen at different times, the tenses have to work together.

Usually common sense kicks in. We combine verbs correctly without giving them much thought. On occasion, though, the juggling is tricky, especially when we throw in *will* or *would.* Here's how to choose between them.

- When the other verb is in the present, use *will*: *Ralph **says** he **will wear** his uniform.*
- When the other verb is in the past, use *would*: *Ralph **said** he **would wear** his uniform.*

The idea is the same with compound tenses, like *has said* (this is called the present perfect) or *had said* (the past perfect).

- When the other verb begins with *has* or *have*, use *will*: *Ralph **has said** he **will need** a bigger size.*
- When the other verb begins with *had*, use *would*: *Ralph **had said** he **would need** a bigger size.*

Another sign of poor tense is using one *have* too many: *He would have liked to have driven a double-decker.* In this case, one *have* is enough, and it can go with either verb, depending on the emphasis: *He would have liked to drive a double-decker*, or *He would like to have driven a double-decker.*

Still tense about tenses? We've only scratched the surface here, so if you need to know more, check your grammar book.

Rules, Schmules

If grammar is supposed to help us make sense, why do some of the rules seem so nonsensical? Well, maybe those aren't real rules, after all.

You've no doubt heard them all your life: Don't split an infinitive. Don't start a sentence with *and* or *but*. Don't end one with a preposition (*of, to, with*, and so on). Don't use contractions (including *don't*). None of them are true—including the one that says *none* is always singular.

These misconceptions, which serve only to make writing clunky and convoluted, are not real rules and never have been. Since the 1300's, writers of English have gotten along fine without them. So where did they come from?

In the eighteenth and nineteenth centuries, classics scholars set out to civilize the English of Chaucer, Shakespeare, and Milton. They took a language that's essentially Germanic and tried to clothe it in Latin grammar. No wonder the shoes pinched.

For generations, our most eminent grammarians have tried to lay these myths and Latinisms to rest, but they keep rising again like Jason from his watery grave. And like Jason, they're not real, so feel free to ignore them. Our best writers do. George Bernard Shaw once complained to the *Times* of London about an editor who hadn't gotten the word:

"There is a pedant on your staff who spends far too much of his time searching for split infinitives. Every good literary craftsman uses a split infinitive if he thinks the sense demands it. I call for this man's instant dismissal; it matters not whether he decides to quickly go or to go quickly or quickly to go. Go he must, and at once."

Comma Sense

I've come across this story many times on the Internet. I can't guarantee that it's true but I still like it. Male and female college students were given these words—*woman without her man is nothing*—and asked to punctuate them as a sentence.

The men wrote: *Woman, without her man, is nothing.*
The women wrote: *Woman: without her, man is nothing.*

Don't overlook the power of punctuation. It's not just window dressing; it can change the meaning of a sentence 180 degrees. This is what I mean: *Jack said Harry wrecked the car.* Or perhaps: *Jack, said Harry, wrecked the car.* And look what a difference a hyphen can make: *The stolen sofa was recovered.* Or: *The stolen sofa was re-covered.*

Sometimes reading a sentence aloud and listening for pauses can help you punctuate it. A slight pause might be a comma; a longer one, a semicolon; an even longer one, a period. (That sentence is an example.) But remember, the point of punctuation is to make writing clearer and easier to read. A barrelful of exclamation marks can't equal one juicy adjective or verb.

I certainly can't tell you in a few paragraphs everything you need to know about punctuation. But I can hit the high spots, the problems that show up most often. If you don't see it here, look it up.

- A comma by itself usually isn't enough to hold together two expressions that could be separate sentences: *Jack broke his crown, Jill wasn't seriously injured.* (This is sometimes called a run-on sentence.) If you want to join those expressions with a comma, add a linking word, like *and* or *but*: *Jack broke his crown, but Jill wasn't seriously injured.* There's more on joining parts of a sentence in chapter 12.
- The semicolon may be the most unappreciated and underused punctuation mark. If you find semicolons intimidating, relax. They're handy for joining expressions that could stand alone, like the ones above: *Jack broke his crown; Jill wasn't seriously injured.* Semicolons can also be used to tidy up a series of items with commas inside

them. Imagine how hard it would be to read this sentence if only commas were used: *Jack broke his crown, which was fractured in two places; scraped his knee, nearly to the bone; and ruined his lederhosen.* Lincoln found the semicolon a "useful little chap"; you will, too.

- Dashes and parentheses shouldn't be abused. They do roughly the same thing—they let the writer say something (like this) in an aside—though dashes are somewhat more in-your-face. If your writing breaks out in dashes, try using parentheses for variety (and vice versa). But if commas would work as well, as they often do, use them instead.

- The exclamation point is a squeal, the "Eek!" of punctuation. It's the equivalent of a flashing neon sign on a sentence. If you're writing something astonishing, remarkable, astounding, or horrific, you'll land a bigger punch by letting your words do the job. A startling statement is all the more startling if it's delivered without an elbow in the ribs. So use exclamation points sparingly. A little punctuation can go a long way.

Incidentally, go easy on the italics. If you have to use slanty print *like this* for emphasis, perhaps your words aren't dramatic enough on their own. It's all right to use italics once in a while, but don't go bananas.

Spellbinding

The most dynamite résumé in the world won't get you in the door if you've misspelled "curriculum vitae." Crummy spelling is more noticeable than crummy anything else. It irritates readers and embarrasses writers. Yet spelling goofs are the easiest to fix. Unless you're dead certain about a word—is it *pretentions* or *pretensions*? *wierd* or *weird*? *gauge* or *guage*?—look it up. Reaching for your Funk & Wagnalls should be a reflex action. Wear it out; thumb it to bits. The best writers I know own the grimiest, most tattered dictionaries.

Dictionaries aren't foolproof, though. Read the fine print when you check the spelling of a word. Lexicographers include troublemakers like *irregardless, alright, ahold,* and *anywheres.* That's because a dictionary is supposed to include words that are widely used, even if they're clearly wrong. But the editors also caution us when these words are nonkosher versions of correct ones (*regardless, all right, a hold, anywhere*). Don't just look up a spelling and stop there; read further, in case it's not the accepted one. Watch for warnings such as "substandard," "nonstandard," "obsolete," "variant spelling," "vulgar," "obscene," and so on.

What about computer spell-checkers? I'm glad you asked. The speller in your machine has a very small IQ and you shouldn't rely on it entirely. First, it may tell you to misspell a word. (Mine doesn't recognize *restaurateur* and tells me to spell it *restauranteur.*) Second, your speller won't stop you from using the wrong word if it's spelled right. (Mine passed this sentence with flying colors: Eye trussed their are know miss steaks hear, four my come pewter is all weighs write.) Third, it's all too easy to hit the wrong key and wreak havoc. On my speller, the Skip Once key is just below Replace. The other day I was ripping through a piece with the spell-checker, repeatedly hitting Skip Once (I thought). But my mouse had drifted up a zillionth of an inch, and I was actually hitting Replace. The discovery prompted me to shout several words that my dictionary describes as "vulgar" or "obscene."

As for grammar-checkers, they've come a long way, but they haven't arrived yet, baby. Like spell-checkers, they overlook many mistakes and encourage you to make many more. There are grammar-checkers that accept "between you and I," "most unique," and "Politics are my favorite subject." When I ran a sentence from the Declaration of Independence through my grammar-checker, it found so many "errors" that I can't list them. Among other things, it suggested changing "all men are created equal" to "God created all men equally." Jefferson would not have approved.

19

Down for the Count

WHEN THE NUMBERS DON'T ADD UP

I once edited a book review in which this sentence appeared (details have been changed to protect the guilty): "Oglethorpe Carrothers was one-third journalist, one-third statesman, one-third war hero, one-third humanitarian, and one-third playboy." Granted, math isn't my strong suit, but I know enough to raise an eyebrow when I meet five-thirds of a Carrothers.

Like that reviewer, many people are more concerned about the sound of their words than the sense of their numbers. The words read well, but the numbers don't add up. Beware of any figures you haven't checked and double-checked. Count on your fingers if you must, but be sure the math makes sense.

Playing the Percentages

What do you make of this sentence? *The stock price jumped 200 percent in less than an hour, rising to $50 from $25.* Something's wrong here (even if you got in on the stock early). Do you see why?

When you start with $25 and you increase that by $25, you've doubled the original figure, to $50. But that's a jump of only 100 percent, the original number increased by itself once. When $25 goes up 200 percent, it increases by itself not once but twice—that gives us the original $25, plus $25 and another $25, for a total of $75.

Goofy percentages whiz past us every day. They routinely appear in newspapers, TV broadcasts, and magazines because nobody stops to count.

Doubling, tripling, and quadrupling are all clear enough: a number is multiplied by two, by three, by four. But tossing in percentages leads to trouble. A number that's doubled goes up 100 percent, a number that's tripled goes up 200 percent, a number that's quadrupled goes up 300 percent, and so on. Go figure.

This is a case where being right isn't necessarily the answer. If there's an alternative, avoid using percentage increases of more than 100, especially big round ones that look wrong even when they're right. It may be correct to write, *Scalpers sold the $10 tickets for $50, **a 400 percent increase**,* but this is better: *Scalpers sold the $10 tickets for $50, **five times the original price**.* When there's no better way, at least make sure the figure is right: *The police arrested 156 scalpers this year, **a 140 percent increase** from the 65 arrested last year.*

Never use *decreases* of more than 100 percent, however, unless you're writing about mathematics. A 100 percent drop gives you zero, so any greater decrease would leave you with a negative number. Outside of math class, your chance of being right is less than zero.

Sorry, Wrong Number

Two times two is four, and that will never change, at least not in our times. But *times* is tricky when you're writing about numbers. What do you make of the calculation here? *Mort owns two Chihuahuas but Rupert owns eight, or four times more.*

If that looks right to you, look again. Rupert actually has *three times more* Chihuahuas than Mort. Think of it this way: Rupert owns six more than Mort. And that's *three times more* than Mort's two, not *four times more.* Chihuahuas don't multiply that fast.

We run into trouble using the expression *times more* when we forget that we're adding the *times* calculation to whatever it's *more* than. The problem is so widespread that I'd suggest ducking it altogether. Why not drop the *more* and use *times as many* or *times as much*? A math teacher— and an English teacher, too—would give you an A for this effort: *Mort owns two Chihuahuas, but Rupert owns eight, or four times as many.*

We also go wrong when we write that a number is umpteen *times less* than another: *Baby Leroy weighs twenty pounds, five times less than his mom, who weighs a hundred.*

The problem is the same; it's just going in the other direction. You could say that the baby weighs *four times less* than his mom (think of it this way: his weight is eighty pounds less, or *four times twenty less*, than his mom's). But even that wording gives me a headache.

Again, I recommend copping out. Drop the *times less* and rephrase the sentence, using *as many as* or *as much as* instead: *Baby Leroy weighs twenty pounds, a fifth as much as his mom, who weighs a hundred.*

The most common *times* problems involve *more* and *less*. But the same principle applies whenever you use numbers to compare things. Instead of saying, *So-and-so is x times richer than what's-his-name*, make it: *So-and-so is x times as rich as what's-his-name* (or *as tall as, as old as,* and so on).

If you take my advice, you'll find it comparatively easy, more or less.

Do Not Fold and Mutilate

How many sheep are in this fold? *Babe's flock of ten sheep increased threefold last year.* No, the answer isn't thirty, although that's probably how most people would interpret the sentence. The answer is forty—the original ten, plus three times that number.

And that's the problem with using *fold* to say how much something has increased. Attaching *fold* to a number is just another way of saying *times*, and it can be just as confusing. Even if you get it right, you'll probably be misunderstood.

The solution? Don't use *fold* to say something has doubled, tripled, or quadrupled. Just say that it has doubled, tripled, or quadrupled: *Babe's flock of ten sheep tripled last year.* Or you could make it: *Babe's flock of ten sheep increased to three times as many last year.* This solution is definitely preferable with larger increases. If Babe ended up with 150 sheep, make it: *Babe's flock of ten sheep increased to fifteen times as many last year.*

By the way, don't use *by* when you mean *to*. They're not the same, not by a long shot. If Babe's flock had increased *by* fifteen times as many, he'd have 160 sheep—the original ten, plus fifteen times as many. Way to go, Babe.

As if *fold* weren't confusing enough, it's even woollier to say, *Babe's flock of ten sheep increased three times last year.* You run into the same problem, and another besides: You might mean that three lambs joined the flock last year, or that the flock increased on three separate occasions.

All right, we've counted enough sheep. One more thing before I fold. Whatever you do, never use *fold* to describe a decrease. I recently read that a country's food supplies had fallen sixfold. If you know what that means, please explain it to me.

Run Those Figures by Me Again

As I've said, I'm not a whiz at math. I make it a practice to check my figures two times, maybe three, with even the most elementary arithmetic. If I get the same number twice, I go with it. But numerically clumsy though I am, I once worked at the *Wall Street Journal*, where every number had to be perfect. If I can get my numbers straight, so can you.

A tip that I learned as a business journalist has stuck with me over the years. It's worth passing on, and it's useful for writing about more than money.

When a number changes, whether it's going up or

going down, it moves from one point to another. So we're tempted to write things like this: *As El Niño arrived, the temperature rose from 5 to 10 degrees.*

But just how warm did it get? The phrase *from 5 to 10* could be read in two ways. It might mean the temperature started at 5 degrees and rose to 10. Or it might mean the increase was between 5 and 10 degrees, so the temperature might have ended up at 40, for example, after beginning somewhere in the 30's.

It's easy to get around this problem. Just put the *to* ahead of the *from*: *As El Niño arrived, the temperature rose to 10 degrees from 5.* Or if you do want to describe an approximate increase, make it: *As El Niño arrived, the temperature rose between 5 and 10 degrees.*

If you keep *to* in front, your readers will know where you're coming *from*.

The Symmetry of Your Digits

I can't promise this problem will be on the SAT's, but it sure comes up a lot: If one in every ten boys starts school early, and three in ten girls, does that mean four out of ten children start school early?

No. If you got it wrong, here's a little remedial math.

First of all, you can't mix the proportions unless there are equal numbers of boys and girls. Assuming that's the case, you don't add the statistics; you average them. If one in ten boys and three in ten girls start school early, then two in every ten children start early.

The principle is the same with percentages. If 8 percent of American men and 12 percent of American women are overweight, that doesn't mean 20 percent of all

American adults are overweight. The answer is 10 percent, again if we assume there are equal numbers of men and women. You don't add the two percentages; you average them. (Remember that if the groups aren't the same size, averaging won't work.)

As with so many other things, the truth lies in between.

When Less Is More

A lot of us can't tell our ups from our downs. If we're comparatively impaired, we might call something a "decrease" when in fact it's an increase—but an increase that's smaller than average, or smaller than last year's, or smaller than expected, or whatever. A lesser increase is still an increase, not a decrease.

Journalists are often guilty of this mistake, especially when they write about budgets. A story on school spending might refer to a "decrease" in maintenance costs when the amount in fact increased—but the increase was smaller than the one expected. As a result, we get a story about "budget cuts" when the budget has actually grown. Sometimes less really *is* more.

Mean Streets

I'll bet the average person doesn't know the difference between *average* and *mean, median* and *norm*, or any of the combinations thereof. The average dictionary may not be of much help, either. Not all dictionaries give precise mathematical meanings.

Imagine you're taking a seminar in desktop publishing. The five students in the class get these scores on their midterm exams: 60, 84, 87, 94, 100. (All right, you're the one who gets 100.) Here's how to find the *average, mean, median,* and *norm.*

- The *average* is 85: the sum of the scores (425) divided by the number of students (5).
- The *mean,* also known as the *arithmetic mean,* is 85: same as *average.* (Some dictionaries and usage guides define *mean* in a looser sense, as the mid-point between extremes.)
- The *median* is 87: the score that falls in the middle when the numbers are arranged by size. If there's an even number of scores, add up the two in the middle and divide by two.
- The *norm* is in the 80's: a less precise term, it's sometimes used to indicate average or median or just "normal"; avoid it when you want to be exact.

If you can remember all that, you're way above average.

Figure Skating

Writers who are careless with figures are on thin ice. What's the weak spot here? *Hundreds of ice fishermen aren't licensed in Minnesota.*

If you don't see what's wrong, here's a clue. Not all ice fishermen are in Minnesota. No doubt there are many thousands, from Maine to Siberia, who aren't licensed to fish in Minnesota. Here's a better way to say it: *Hundreds of ice fishermen in Minnesota aren't licensed.*

When you write with numbers, be sure your wording isn't misleading. Readers may guess what you mean, but why should they have to? If there's any ambiguity, rearrange the words, as in the example above, or add any information that may be missing. Something's missing here: *Seven out of ten people are robbed by someone they know.*

I doubt it. Most people are never robbed by anyone, strangers or otherwise. Say it this way: *Seven out of ten people robbed are victims of someone they know.*

Statistics can be treacherous. As Disraeli supposedly said: "There are three kinds of lies: lies, damned lies, and statistics."

PART 3

Getting Better All the Time

egugihfewyendjimocisjetwirikidoirieindtwyki
jghrtgerfdtsyhejuogehtrysfertdgwrsteyhfushke
dhtjncgeykiduwournhrsgeyifkdleystqnnaqmmxusdn
ojste eujnflksmcdafewdurheksjfredhulisfd
lryusfetrdgshuwyrtghsyeturheydfgj
hrtegsfdytjhrjuktjfgersfegydthmburfdgsyegfhsuyef

20

Lost Horizon

WHAT'S THE POINT OF VIEW?

From where I sit, it's easy to look up from my writing and glance out the window. Much too easy. A short glance can turn into a long, lingering gaze. A reverie, even. That's why I draw the curtains when I start to write. I'm more likely to stay focused on my work if I can't look away.

I want my readers to stay focused, too. I want them to look where I want them to look, to see what I want them to see. To control what and how a reader sees, a writer controls the point of view, or perspective.

If you're writing a job résumé, for instance, you'll want to mention your award for community service, but not the time you got busted for disorderly conduct. That's using perspective. As you can see, point of view is more than just the voice a writer uses to address readers—personal or impersonal or somewhere in between. By limiting what readers know, point of view influences what they think.

In simple, straightforward writing, like a thank-you note or a quick e-mail, we don't need to worry much about perspective. But when the writing is more complicated—a long article, a story or a novel, a piece on a sensitive subject, anything intended to persuade—the point of view becomes more of an issue.

Whether you realize it or not, everything you write has a perspective. And you change perspective all the time, perhaps without even knowing it. For starters, your point of view shifts whenever you use an anecdote or a funny story at the beginning of an essay, a speech, a short story, or any other kind of writing. When you begin with something specific or personal and then move to a wider topic, you've changed perspective.

Remember that readers can go only where you take them. If your point of view is jerky or inconsistent, if it's not clear or convincing, they'll lose their way. No matter what you're writing and no matter who your readers are, they need to know where they are and why: Whose voice is this? Whose opinions are these? Whose shoes am I standing in? Where am I supposed to be looking? These are questions about point of view.

Get Some Perspective

We've all been fooled by card tricks. The hand may not be quicker than the eye, but when the cards are moved around often enough, it certainly seems that way. If you don't want your readers to get lost in the shuffle, don't move your cards around too quickly.

When a writer switches point of view for no good reason, readers become disoriented. A case in point: *As Leo gazed longingly into her blue-gray eyes, Molly realized he was standing on her foot.*

Sentences like that remind me of an old record album, *How Can You Be in Two Places at Once When You're Not Anywhere at All?* There's no reason to jump from Leo's point of view to Molly's. The result is a yo-yo quality. Make it: *As Leo gazed longingly into Molly's blue-gray eyes, he didn't realize he was standing on her foot.* That way Molly is the only one who's uncomfortable.

Easy Does It

I learned to drive on a stick shift, and the car protested loudly until I got the hang of it. Shifting smoothly takes practice, in writing as well as in driving. A clumsy shift in perspective can be as grating as the sound of grinding gears.

Even when there are many things to describe, it's possible to move from one to another smoothly. Say we're writing about a busy harbor town in a piece for a travel magazine. We start out small, with a particular red fishing boat bobbing at anchor. Then we pull back, describing the pattern all the brightly colored boats make on the blue water. We pull back farther still, to include some gulls overhead, then the wharves at the foot of the village, then the bustling dockside street, then the houses extending up the hill and thinning out as they get farther from the water. Notice how the perspective shifts smoothly, moving from small to large, from particular to general, like a zoom lens on a camera.

Then let's say we add the fact that the red fishing boat has nets spread on its deck, drying in the sun. Crash! There we were, hovering somewhere in the sky above the village, when the bottom dropped out.

Be kind to readers. Let them down gently.

The More Things Change

Once you're aware of how perspective works, you can use it in a special way. You can organize a long piece of writing, even an unwieldy one, by alternating the points of view.

Suppose you have to prepare an article about the discovery of some primitive cave paintings. You have piles of material, falling roughly into two categories. On the one hand you have your own observations about the site, the scientists involved, and the details of the discovery. On the other you have more general information about the history of the region and its people, the evolution of ancient art, and other background material.

You might organize your article by alternating the two points of view. You could begin by describing the site as you saw it, then pull back to fill in some history, zoom in on the scientists as you witness their big find, zoom out again to include something about the artistic development of primitive people, then back in to the scene and efforts to preserve the paintings.

This method of switching perspectives—from near to far, general to specific, personal to impersonal—has long been used by fiction writers, not only to change the point of view from character to character, but also to alternate scenes in the present with flashbacks to the past.

The technique has become popular with nonfiction writers, too. It works so well as a means of organization that you'll find it in books and articles of every conceivable kind. It's popular because it works. But it works only if the shifts in perspective are graceful.

An effective way to shift smoothly from one perspective to another is to bridge the points of view with a common element. If you're writing a profile of a present-day farm family, for instance, you might change your subject and your perspective by ending one paragraph and beginning the next like this:

Gunnar Bjornstrand surveyed his parched field one last time, then idly picked up a fistful of earth and let it run through his fingers.

It was the rich, black soil of Potawatomi County that had drawn Scandinavian immigrants to the area 150 years earlier.

That shift is a big one in viewpoint and in time, but it doesn't jar the reader. In this case, the gap between the parts has been bridged by a common image, the soil.

You don't have to use a common element to move smoothly from one perspective to another. What matters is that the shift makes some sort of sense. A reader who can't see why the perspective has changed will feel like a tennis ball being whacked from court to court.

The Beast in the Jungle

In a piece of fiction, the change in perspective is often unintrusive, especially when the writer wants to interrupt the action as little as possible. There's a neat shift in Hemingway's story "The Short Happy Life of Francis Macomber." The setting is an African safari, and we join it in mid-paragraph. In this passage, we see the hunt first through the eyes of a wounded lion as he's shot a second time, and later through the eyes of the hunter:

"Then it crashed again and he felt the blow as it hit his lower ribs and ripped on through, blood sudden hot and frothy in his mouth, and he galloped toward the high grass where he could crouch and not be seen and make them bring the crashing thing close enough so he could make a rush and get the man that held it.

"Macomber had not thought how the lion felt as he got out of the car. He only knew his hands were shaking and as he walked away from the car it was almost impossible for him to make his legs move."

Maybe we can't write like Hemingway, but we can try to shift gently so readers won't hear the gears grinding.

Name That Tone

You're watching a horror movie, maybe *Friday the 13th, Part VIII*, but with the sound track from *Mary Poppins*. Should you scream, or laugh?

If a writer's tone doesn't match the point of view, readers won't know what to think. You wouldn't begin a funeral oration with a vaudeville joke, unless you were burying Henny Youngman, or write about what a bummer life is when you're trying to cheer up a depressed friend.

You can't maintain a clear point of view without a consistent tone. If your attitude is inappropriate, or if it veers around for no good reason—from tragic to flippant, sympathetic to hostile, optimistic to despairing—the perspective gets confused, and so does the reader. I think that's one reason we seldom read convincing fiction with a deranged person as the narrator.

Since your tone is part of your point of view, don't change one without changing the other. And when you do change your tone, be clear about it. This is another case where you have to put yourself in the readers' minds. What will they think? How will they feel? Is that what you want them to be thinking or feeling?

Your choice of words can make a tremendous difference in tone. Say you have to write a campaign ad criticizing one politician and praising another, though the two hardly differ (it's been known to happen). Your mission, obviously, is to send out good vibes for your guy and bad vibes for the competition. Here's how minor differences in wording can convey an approving tone for Tweedledum and a disapproving tone for Tweedledee.

Suppose both candidates are windbags whose most recent speeches lasted not quite sixty minutes. You might write that Tweedledum spoke for *barely an hour*, while Tweedledee spoke for *nearly an hour*.

Perhaps both support new programs costing just under $2 million. Your candidate's program would cost *less than $2 million*. The other candidate's would cost *almost $2 million* or *upward of $2 million*.

Astoundingly, both candidates have changed their positions to fit the polls. Tweedledum is *flexible* or *responsive*, naturally, but Tweedledee *waffles* on the issues.

Both have failed to live up to previous campaign promises. Your guy has *moderated* his expectations, while the opponent has *fallen short*. Your candidate *acknowledges* a weakness while the other *admits* to one. You get the idea.

Even a change in word order can affect your tone. Let's say both candidates have a history of stiffing their creditors. Tweedledum *may once have declared bankruptcy, but he now practices fiscal responsibility*. Tweedledee *may now practice fiscal responsibility, but he once declared bankruptcy*. Saying the same thing from a different perspective can convey a different tone, subtly or not so subtly.

Politicians, not to mention lobbyists, advertisers, and anyone else trying to persuade, regularly manipulate facts to achieve a particular tone. Is this fair? Well, I'd like to say that the material should decide the tone, not the other way around. But to some extent all writers manipulate the facts, simply by the choices they make in presenting their material.

Unless you have an ax to grind, be as honest as you can with readers. Try to let your tone emerge naturally from your content. When material that's supposed to be straightforward is manipulated to create a certain effect, the writing can sound strained and artificial.

All writing has an attitude. Make sure yours is right for your material.

21

Wimping Out

THE BACKWARD WRITER

Indirect writing is a limp handshake with the reader. It's speaking out of the corner of your mouth. It's refusing to look the reader in the eye. It's weak, evasive, and dishonest, and in some fields—business, politics, public relations, advertising—it's a skill that's been elevated to an art.

People say things indirectly for many reasons. Some think a simple idea is more impressive if it sounds complicated. Some express themselves in a convoluted way because they think it's required of them. Some like to sugarcoat unpalatable facts. Some are covering up holes in their arguments. Some don't want to tell the whole truth. Some are timid. And some simply don't know how to be direct.

What do these roundabout writers do instead? They back into their statements, they pile on jargon or obfuscatory words (*obfuscatory* is one), or they use passive verbs. They bob and weave but never land a punch.

Take a simple, direct sentence like *Cyril shot Sir Cedric.* You can't get more up-front than that. It says who did what, and to whom. But a writer who wants to avoid mentioning the guilty party (Cyril's defense attorney, perhaps) might use a passive verb: *Sir Cedric was shot.* Someone who doesn't want to be specific (a police detective, for instance) could use officialese: *Sir Cedric was the victim of a homicide.* The bureaucrat who likes to water things down might use a weak noun instead of a strong verb: *A shooting took place.* And a truly evasive writer could score a hat trick by using all these methods at once: *Sir Cedric's shooting is being treated as a homicide.*

Notice how tame and bloodless those sentences sound compared with the original. Sir Cedric was shot, all right, but not by anybody in particular. The culprit, if there is one, has left the building.

The difference between direct and indirect writing is the difference between witnessing the murder and finding the body. Get to know indirect writing when you see it, and root it out of your own work. Now for a closer look at some of the guises indirect writing can take.

No Officialese, Please

A lot of people, among them bureaucrats and academics, are fond of what my grandfather referred to as "two-dollar words." These indirect writers use inflated language—

otherwise known as bureaucratese, officialese, academese, or jargon—to avoid saying something unpleasant, perhaps to make themselves sound important, or to cloak a weak argument in what Churchill called "terminological inexactitude."

You know the old maxim "If you can't say something nice, don't say anything at all"? Evasive writers can usually find a way to say something unpleasant without coming right out with it. They'd rather not say anything, but if forced to make a statement they'll back into it by using officialese.

A spokesman for a toxic-waste refinery says, *Twelve fatalities occurred,* not *Twelve people died.* As your plane sits on the runway, the pilot announces, *We are experiencing difficulty in identifying the cause of the malfunction,* not *We don't know what's wrong.*

Jargon is also handy for dressing up a simple idea. A literary critic who likes to put on airs might praise an author's *unique enunciatory modality* instead of her originality. A dogcatcher who wants to sound important might call himself a *canine control coordinator.*

Unless you have a good reason to be evasive, avoid officialese. For one thing, when you're fudging you use up more words; that's reason enough to be direct. For another, pompous, bureaucratic writing can make you sound dishonest even when you're not. (You'll find more on jargon in chapter 6.)

Noun Proliferation

A wishy-washy writer uses weak nouns (like *destruction*) instead of strong verbs (like *destroy*). The wimp writes,

*The storm resulted in the **destruction** of the building*, instead of *The storm **destroyed** the building*.

If you sense something soft and mushy in your writing, check for a verb that's been nouned. There's no better way to blunt the force of a verb. Make it: *Trollope **wrote** the book in six months.* Not: *The **writing** of the book took Trollope six months.* Make it: *Judge Crater **disappeared** mysteriously.* Not: *Judge Crater's **disappearance** was mysterious.*

Wimpy nouns are creeping into all kinds of writing. Don't let them creep into yours.

Passive-Aggressive

There's no getting away from anemic writing. We hear it routinely on the evening news. When a big shot in an expensive suit acknowledges that *mistakes **were made*** instead of confessing, *I **made** mistakes*, he's being indirect. There's no guilty party, just a vacant chair.

That kind of indirect writing—the passive variety—is easy to spot. It reverses the usual order of subject (*I*), verb (*made*), object (*mistakes*), so that we get the object first, elevated to a subject (*mistakes*), followed by a passive verb (*were made*). What's missing is the "real" subject, the responsible party. Pretty neat, huh?

When we state the case directly, we put the blame where it belongs. When we use a passive verb to disguise the true subject, the culprit gets off scot-free. This is why a passive verb can be the next best thing to a lie. Technically you're telling the truth, though backhandedly. But you're concealing an important piece of information: whodunit. (Granted, that's sometimes the intent.)

Some writers, called on to choose between an active verb and a passive, will choose the passive every time. They'll write, *It is believed that* . . . , instead of saying who believes it, or *He's been called a* . . . , instead of saying who called him one. Cowards! Maybe a writer who can't or won't identify the real subject shouldn't say anything at all.

Of course, writing backward is not inherently evil. Overboard let us not go. You might have good reason to use a passive verb if (1) you don't want to say who's responsible, (2) you don't know, (3) it's not important, or (4) you're saving a surprise for the end. Some examples:

An irregularity has been brought to my attention. You'd rather not say who snitched.

Brussels is said to be dull. You can't cite an authority.

Cyril was handcuffed and led away. Obviously, the cops put on the cuffs.

Lefty was strangled with his own suspenders. The weapon is the surprise.

But try not to use passive verbs if you don't need to. There's an element of accountability in an active verb that's often lacking in a passive one. An active verb makes somebody or something responsible for an action. So don't weasel into a sentence from the wrong end. Examine your writing and change passive verbs into active ones where you can. You'll sound more authoritative, less mealy-mouthed. Besides, it's a more responsible way to write.

When you write indirectly—with passive verbs, pompous words, or corkscrew sentences—you turn away from the reader. (Another kind of evasion, the back-door denial, is discussed in chapter 27.) If you have nothing to hide, don't chicken out. When you have something to say, look the reader in the eye and say it.

egúyinrewyendjfmocisjectwnfkiaofrrerndtwykt
jghrtgerfdtsyhejuogehtrysfertdgwrsteyhfushkey
dhtjncgerhiduwournhrsgeyifkdleystqnnaqmmxusdni
ojste   teujnflksmcdafewdurheksjfredhulisfd
lryusfetrdgshuwyrtghsyeturheydfgj
hrtegsfdytjhrjuktjfgersfegydthmburfdgsyegfhsuyef

22

Everybody's Favorite Subject

I, ME, MY

There's an old gag about a guy who rattles on and on about himself, oblivious of anyone else's existence. "But enough about me," he finally says. "What do *you* think of my hair weave?"

Everybody knows that blowhard, or someone like him. And that may be why many of us find it hard to write in the first person. We cringe at the thought of coming across as vain or boastful, especially if we're self-conscious to begin with. We imagine weary readers drumming their fingers, rolling their eyes, checking the clock, and thinking, "What an ego!"

Meanwhile, just as many of us find it easy, much too easy, to use the first person. We bask in the warmth of our own regard. Our favorite pronouns are *I*, *me*, and *my*. Hey, there's enough of Number One to go around, isn't there? Why not be generous? Here's looking at *me*, kid.

I used to belong to the first group, the shy ones (no wisecracks, please). I wasn't always the self-assured extrovert you see before you. It took me years to feel comfortable in the first person. In fact, I still get a twinge every once in a while (like now), wondering whether I'm being too *my*-opic.

Song of Myself

If you're one of the shy ones, be brave. Give yourself permission to come onstage and write in the first person. It's intimate. It lets you speak to the reader one-on-one. Best of all, the first person lets you write about the subject you know best—you.

If you're writing a memoir, an autobiography, or a letter, you'll naturally want to speak for yourself. And fiction writers, too, as we'll see, quite often choose the first person. But many other kinds of prose—speeches, reports, essays, reviews, to name a few—may lend themselves to the personal touch as well. Some things simply work better in the first person, like this scathing rejection of Proust's *Remembrance of Things Past*:

"I may perhaps be dead from the neck up, but rack my brains as I may I can't see why a chap should need thirty pages to describe how he turns over in bed before going to sleep."

Whether or not you agree with the sentiment, you have

to admit that the French editor who wrote it was right to choose the first person. By all means use it when there's a reason—to sharpen a barb, to soften a blow, to take responsibility for a statement, to get personal with the reader.

But if you're hooked on the first person and can't produce a sentence without yourself in it, you have a problem. Don't let the air out of your ego just yet, though. You'll need it later. Step back a few paces. Think of your readers. Do they need your opinion, or can the facts stand on their own? Is your presence helping, or is it an obstacle that readers must navigate around? Be honest. This calls for a cold eye. Since it's always easier to be ruthless with somebody else's writing, be critical as you imagine sitting through this speech:

> *As I stand here today, I thank you for offering me the grave challenge of addressing this graduating class on the future of our youth in America. I profoundly believe, and history will no doubt bear me out, that the youngsters of today will be the adults of tomorrow. But I ask myself this question: Will there be a tomorrow? I am of the opinion, and I'm sure you will agree with me, that only America's youth can answer my question. As you decide whether to cast your lot with the past or the future, remember the words I have spoken here: The day after today, as I see it, is just another way of saying tomorrow.*

Now imagine that same speech, but with less of the speaker in it:

> *Thank you for offering me the grave challenge of addressing this graduating class on the future of youth in America. History will show that the youngsters of*

*today will be the adults of tomorrow. But will there
be a tomorrow? Only America's youth can answer
that. As you decide whether to cast your lot with the
past or the future, remember that the day after today
is just another way of saying tomorrow.*

Well, it's still empty twaddle, but at least it's less self-important. One problem at a time. By weeding out unnecessary first-person singulars (*I, me, my, mine, myself*), we let readers know that we're thinking more of them and less of ourselves.

I'm Out of Here

Deciding where you belong—onstage or behind the scenes—isn't always simple. When does a travel article become an ego trip? A modest proposal, an advertisement for *myself*? You may be happy to learn that in many kinds of writing, the decision isn't up to you.

Where objectivity—or at least the appearance of it—is important, the first person is discouraged or greatly restricted. This is especially true with newspapers and newsmagazines. A reporter covering hard news (a coup d'état, say, or a vote in Congress) is supposed to remain in the background and let the facts speak for themselves. Even the occasional personal comment is often given in the third person: *This correspondent heard heavy artillery* or *Heavy artillery was heard*, instead of *I heard heavy artillery*.

Manipulative writers, however, can slant the news without resorting to the first person. In fact, they'll avoid it like the plague. Why get personal and alert readers that opinions are coming? There goes the illusion of impartiality. A few first-person intrusions would tip off even the sleepiest reader:

The House of Representatives voted unanimously today to increase salaries of members of Congress by 75 percent. **I can't wait to see the polls.** *The bill's sponsors mustered bipartisan support for the measure.* **I'll just bet they did!** *Sponsors argued—this slays me—that existing salary levels might prohibit all but the wealthy from running for office.* **Tell me another one.**

Okay, that's an exaggerated example. The point is that first-person writing is generally frowned on in the news pages (though not in columns, reviews, features, and analyses).

Other places where *I, me,* and *my* aren't always welcome include scientific and academic journals and corporate and government reports. For the most part, such writing is deliberately impersonal, even if that makes it dry and indirect.

My husband once helped a French scientist translate a research paper into English. It emerged so clear, simple, and direct that no scientific journal wanted it. The paper had to be rewritten in formal academese—dense, impersonal, and indirect—before it could be published.

Here are some of the ways scientists make *I* disappear:

• They use *one* instead: *Subtracting the magnetic moment of the neutron from that of the proton,* **one** *observes that the Heisenberg principle is an inverse function of the Planck effect.*

- They use *we*: *The equation changes when **we** expand this definition to include Bohr's hypothesis.*
- They replace *I* with *the author*: *In this study, **the author** has attempted to show that magnetic moment bears an occipital relationship to acceleration squared.*
- They use a passive verb: *As **will be demonstrated**, chaos theory undermines the dynamics of the Lorentz measurements.*

You don't like this kind of writing? Well, I don't either. My instincts tell me to avoid indirect writing, but the choice isn't always up to me. And it won't always be up to you. What's the lesson? If readers want impersonal, give them impersonal. Hold your nose if you must, but accept that the audience you're writing for is always right.

If you have to be impersonal but you don't want to sound dry and remote, try this. Write a rough draft in the first person, then go through and take out every *I*, *me*, and *my*. You may have to tinker here and there, but it's worth the trouble. By the way, those first three methods scientists use to avoid *I* and company aren't quite as bloodless as the fourth, where there's nobody in the picture at all.

To be fair, the first person is often inappropriate in a formal academic paper, and not just because of its informal tone. *I*, *me*, and *my* can make an argument look weaker, as if it's based on opinion instead of evidence: *In **my judgment**, Abélard is not a tragic figure. **It appears to me** that he is one more example of the irresponsible clergyman. By seducing Héloïse, fathering a son, and secretly marrying her, **I believe**, he determined his own fate. **I think** that's why* *he is remembered today more for his love letters than for his theological writings.*

If you write like that, hedging your bets, you'll sound as though you don't have confidence in your argument. When you have a case you believe in, don't emasculate it.

Some Facts about Fiction

Fiction writers are often more comfortable, more themselves, in the first person. Beginners seem to find it natural to write in the voice of a character. But they're not alone. Some of literature's greatest novels have first-person narrators: *Jane Eyre* ("Reader, I married him"), *Great Expectations* ("The man, after looking at me for a moment, turned me upside down, and emptied my pockets"), *The Adventures of Huckleberry Finn* ("I felt so lonesome I most wished I was dead"), *Moby-Dick* ("When I go to sea, I go as a simple sailor").

Be warned, though. Using the first person may be the easiest way to begin a work of fiction and the hardest way to finish one. Limiting yourself to one character's point of view can make it difficult to be everywhere you want to be and say everything you want to say.

A first-person narrator can't see around corners or through walls; only an omniscient narrator (one who's all-knowing and all-seeing) can. An individual character can't know other characters' thoughts; only an omniscient narrator can. If what you're writing requires godlike knowledge of everything and everyone, the first person won't work.

Say you're planning a story about a young couple's visit to the obstetrician, and you want to write it entirely from the husband's point of view. If he's in the waiting room while the doctor and the patient are in the examining room, you can't very well describe the doctor listening through the stethoscope—unless you're writing science fiction and the prospective dad has X-ray vision.

An extremely skilled novelist, however, can write in the first person and still tell the reader things the narrator doesn't know. I'm thinking of Kazuo Ishiguro's *The Remains of the Day*, a novel seen through the eyes of a butler with blinkered vision. The narrator himself is unaware of the emotional and political turmoil around him, but through him the reader sees what he doesn't.

In one episode, Stevens, the butler, reminisces about Lord Darlington, the nobleman he devotedly served for thirty-five years, and about the importance of well-polished silver in the running of a great household. "I am glad to be able to recall numerous occasions when the silver at Darlington Hall had a pleasing impact upon observers," he says.

As he talks about the silver, we learn little by little that something much more serious was happening at Darlington Hall back in the 1930's—a meeting between a British Cabinet minister, Lord Halifax, and a Nazi diplomat, Herr Ribbentrop.

"But then at one point I overheard Lord Halifax exclaiming: 'My goodness, Darlington, the silver in this house is a delight.' I was of course very pleased to hear this at the time, but what was for me the truly satisfying corollary to this episode came two or three days later, when Lord Darlington remarked to me: 'By the way, Stevens,

Lord Halifax was jolly impressed with the silver the other night. Put him into a quite different frame of mind altogether.' These were—I recollect it clearly—his lordship's actual words and so it is not simply my fantasy that the state of the silver had made a small, but significant contribution towards the easing of relations between Lord Halifax and Herr Ribbentrop that evening."

The unwitting narrator sees only the world reflected in his exquisitely polished silver. But between the lines, readers learn that his adored employer, Lord Darlington, has been secretly furthering Hitler's cause among leading figures in the British government.

Not all writers can pull that off. If you'd like to try, read as much first-person fiction as you can, and pay attention to what's going on. Some wonderful first-person writing is layered and complex, like the passage above, and some is more straightforward. But all of it has a feeling of inevitability, as though it couldn't have been written in any other way. It's hard to imagine Ralph Ellison's *Invisible Man*, the story of a young black man's struggle for identity, in anything but the first person:

"I am an invisible man. No, I am not a spook like those who haunted Edgar Allan Poe; nor am I one of your Hollywood-movie ectoplasms. I am a man of substance, of flesh and bone, fiber and liquids—and I might even be said to possess a mind. I am invisible, understand, simply because people refuse to see me."

That feeling of alienation, of barely suppressed anguish, wouldn't come across if the passage had been written in the third person. See for yourself. Try replacing every *I* with a *he*. Do the same thing when you have doubts about your own writing. Strip each *I*, *me*, and *my* from an important passage. If it collapses, the first person is the right choice. If your presence isn't called for, get out.

But enough about you.

Promises, Promises

MAKING THEM, KEEPING THEM

Every playwright knows you don't put a gun onstage unless you intend to use it. That's a good rule to follow, no matter what kind of writing you do. A careless hint or a subject that's raised and then dropped is a gun left in plain view but never fired. It's a promise to the audience— "Trust me to deliver the goods"—that's never kept.

A writer makes promises to keep the reader reading (or the audience awake). The promises can be quite obvious, like saying you have a major announcement to make, or more subtle, like the gun that leaves folks wondering when it will go off.

A promise is anything that piques interest and begs for explanation: *As we shall see, his failure to test the bungee cords was to have tragic consequences.* Or: *Leona bailed out at $13 a share, a decision she would later regret.* Or: *They kissed outside the cryogenics lab, vowing to meet again in a better world, but it was not to be.*

Even small details can be promises. You might begin a profile of a corporate executive by describing her office, littered with promises: a wheelchair in one corner, a stuffed sailfish on the wall, a half-eaten jelly doughnut on the desk. Every promise raises a question. Is that her wheelchair? If so, what happened? Did she land that fish? Is she going to finish the doughnut? Readers will keep reading because they want to know.

And you have to tell them. An audience has the memory of an elephant. Never raise expectations you don't plan to meet. You might forget a casual teaser, but readers won't. And what you see as an insignificant aside (*He knew he had to fix that step one of these days*) might seem a portent to your readers. Don't leave them hanging.

Suppose you're writing a magazine article on dry-cleaning methods and you mention that you were furious when your marabou boa came back from the cleaner's. Readers will expect to be told why. Or you're giving a speech on exotic pets and you happen to recall warning your late brother-in-law not to hand-feed his crocodile. The audience will expect to hear the rest of the story, so keep your promise.

Those of you with attention deficit disorder may need nudging, especially if you're writing something long. Jot down a note whenever you make a promise in your writing—when you mention a subject or refer to an incident you plan to pick up later. Stick your reminder in an obvious place, on a wall or bulletin board or at the edge of your computer terminal. Any loose ends should be tied up eventually.

Our reading, both fiction and nonfiction, is full of promises that hint at where we're going and help move us along. Since we could be going almost anywhere, a promise can hint at almost anything, from unusual plot twists to a startling scientific discovery.

A promise or two at the beginning of a book can give readers a taste of what's to come:

> "How did our Sun come into being, what keeps it hot and luminous, and what will be its ultimate fate?"
> (George Gamow,
> *The Birth and Death of the Sun*)

> "This is the saddest story I have ever heard."
> (Ford Madox Ford, *The Good Soldier*)

> "Benjamin Disraeli's career was an extraordinary one; but there is no need to make it seem more extraordinary than it really was."
> (Robert Blake, *Disraeli*)

A promise at the end of a chapter can engage readers and make them turn the page. In these examples, the promise is a note of suspense:

"As the year of 1931 ran its uneasy course, with five
million wage earners out of work, the middle
classes facing ruin, the farmers unable to meet
their mortgage payments, the Parliament paralyzed, the government floundering, the eighty-
four-year-old President fast sinking into the
befuddlement of senility, a confidence mounted
in the breasts of the Nazi chieftains that they
would not have long to wait."

(William L. Shirer,
The Rise and Fall of the Third Reich)

"Halfway down I paused and leaned on the hand-
rail and told myself that I was descending into
trouble: a pretty young woman with a likable boy
and a wandering husband. A hot wind was blow-
ing in my face."

(Ross Macdonald, *The Underground Man*)

"The truth about his new American correspondent
was a great deal stranger than this detached, inno-
cent, and otherworldly Scotsman could have ever
imagined."

(Simon Winchester,
The Professor and the Madman)

"It would be many hours before I learned that
everything had not in fact turned out great—that
nineteen men and women were stranded up on
the mountain by the storm, caught in a desperate
struggle for their lives."

(Jon Krakauer, *Into Thin Air*)

Promises can put readers on the alert that something important is about to happen. In these passages, hints of ominous doings create a sense of foreboding:

"Now I thought: There's going to be trouble here."
(V. S. Naipaul, *A Bend in the River*)

"So do not forget this Marvin Macy, as he is to act a terrible part in the story which is yet to come."
(Carson McCullers, *The Ballad of the Sad Café*)

"From my father I inherited an optimism which did not leave me until recently."
(Joan Didion, *Play It as It Lays*)

"Like the waters of the river, like the motorists on the highway, and like the yellow trains streaking down the Santa Fe tracks, drama, in the shape of exceptional happenings, had never stopped there."
(Truman Capote, *In Cold Blood*)

Promises are glue, gripping the reader's attention by holding a long piece of writing together. A good writer can juggle three or four or more promises at once, so there's always something else the reader wants to know, another reason not to switch off the light and go to bed.

Some promises, though, are subtle; the reader recognizes them only in retrospect. They may be as unobtrusive as a recurring image, like the umbrellas that pop up at fateful moments in *Madame Bovary*. Flaubert's first mention of an umbrella comes early in the novel, when the

local priest tells the innkeeper he's left his umbrella behind
and asks that it be sent on to him. That same evening, the
Bovarys arrive in town. They dine at the inn, and then a
servant carrying the curé's umbrella shows them to their
new home. Later, Emma Bovary will buy her lover a present from an umbrella shop, a costly gift that she has to
steal from her husband to pay for. And still later, she secretly meets another lover in a raging storm. As lightning
flashes around them, they embrace and kiss—under an
umbrella.

Whether they're subtle or not so subtle, promises
make a book worth reading again and again because they
seem more meaningful with each reading. As you read and
as you write, think about promises and keep your eye on
the ball—or the umbrella. And anytime you raise the
reader's expectations, remember that you have promises to
keep.

24

You Got Rhythm

WRITING TO THE BEAT

Mention rhythm and most people think of music: hip-hop, polka, fugue, march, waltz, rockabilly. But almost everything in life has rhythm, from your heartbeat to the clickety-clack of your keyboard, from a jackhammer in the street to rain drumming on the roof. And your writing has it, too.

By "rhythm" I don't mean just the toe-tapping beat created by the rise and fall of syllables as word follows word. I mean all the patterns in writing: the sound of words and phrases, figures of speech, rhymes, repetition, and so on. Taken together, these give a piece of writing its flow, its stride, its timing—that's rhythm.

Open a book, any book, and start reading aloud. Forget for a moment what the words mean. Just listen to the rhythm. Is it jerky because the phrases are short and choppy? Is it leisurely because the clauses are long and drawn out? Does the monotony of the cadences make you drowsy? Does the pulsating drive get your adrenaline going?

It should come as no surprise that language has rhythm. Our first acquaintance with it, after all, is through our ears. As children we hear language before we can understand and speak it; we speak before we can read; we read before we can write. And the language we write has something of the language we hear—the quality of rhythm.

We know that poetry has rhythm. So does prose, though its rhythms may not be as obvious. Great prose writers have always used rhythm to give their words another dimension. We mere mortals may not be able to do that. But when we're trying to write our best—in a love letter, a short story, an essay for admission to medical school—we should make sure that our rhythms don't detract from our words.

Not everything has to sing, of course. If you're writing a recipe or instructions for assembling a tricycle or dosage directions for an aspirin label, rhythm may not be your first consideration. Readers won't mind monotony or a bump or two, as long as the facts are right. A lot depends on how much time you have to fuss. A reporter covering a plane crash on deadline won't play around with rhythm as much as someone writing a feature story about the birth of a panda. Then again, rhythm may not be as critical in a news story that has its own excitement and drama.

Snooze Alarm

The most important lesson about rhythm is also the easiest to learn: Too much of it may put the reader to sleep. And that's the last thing you want to do, unless you're writing bedtime stories. A repetitive rhythm can have a hypnotic effect, lulling readers instead of holding their attention. This is the kind of writing I mean:

In the still of the night, a crack in the floor caught the heel of Mae's shoe, and she fell down the stairs of the rickety house. The bump in the dark put a limp in her walk and a run in her hose, but it didn't disturb a hair on her head.

Are you thoroughly anesthetized? The problem with the passage is that too many phrases (*still of the night, heel of Mae's shoe, crack in the floor*) have the same rhythm. Two or three similar phrases may be all right, but a long string of them becomes monotonous. The solution is easy. Break up the singsong pattern by changing a few words or moving them around:

In the dead of night, Mae's heel caught on a crack in the floor of the rickety house and she tumbled down the stairs. The fall tore her stocking and left her with a limp, but it didn't disturb a hair on her head.

Can you hear the difference? There are still a few phrases with similar cadences, yet the overall rhythm isn't sleep-inducing. Don't be obsessive about avoiding repetitive rhythms. Use them but don't abuse them, particularly if you're trying to convey excitement or tension.

Out of Sync

Here's Irritating Situation Number 47. You're in a romantic restaurant, enjoying an intimate meal with your one-and-only, when some jerk at the next table starts shouting into a cell phone. Kind of spoils the ambience, doesn't it? A piece of writing can be spoiled, too, if its rhythm is out of sync with its content.

Imagine you're the president of a family-owned company beset by rumors that it's about to close and everybody's going to be laid off. Your object is to assure employees that the rumors are false and that their jobs are safe. You draft an e-mail statement like this:

> *Dear friends: You're upset. Of course you are, and we are too! Who wouldn't be? The rumor mill is out of control. But all the loose talk is untrue. This company is not closing. It's doing well financially. Sales are up. No one's being laid off. We expect to be in business for many years to come. And we hope you'll all be here.*

That doesn't sound very soothing, does it? The choppy rhythm gives the writing a nervous edge, and the employees are nervous enough as it is. So let's fiddle with the rhythm:

> *Dear friends: We're just as upset as you are over false rumors about our company's future. None of them are true. In fact, our sales are up, business is good, and we're doing well financially. So there's no reason we*

would close or let anyone go. We'll be here for many
years to come, and we hope you'll be here with us.

The first version could have been written by Barney
Fife, the jumpy deputy on *The Andy Griffith Show*. The
second one sounds more like the laid-back Sheriff Taylor.

Sometimes, though, an edgy, percussive rhythm
might be just what you're after. In *Miami and the Siege of
Chicago*, Norman Mailer describes demonstrators during
the 1968 Democratic National Convention, and he does it
in a marching cadence, one that swells along with the
crowd:

"In broken ranks, half a march, half a happy mob, eyes
red from gas, faces excited by the tension of the afternoon,
and the excitement of the escape from Grant Park, now
pushing down Michigan Avenue toward the Hilton Hotel
with dreams of a march on to the Amphitheatre four miles
beyond, and in the full pleasure of being led by the wagons
of the Poor People's March, the demonstrators shouted to
everyone on the sidewalk, 'Join us, join us, join us,' and the
sidewalk kept disgorging more people ready to march."

In that single sentence we feel the sting of the tear gas,
hear the wagons rolling, and see the march growing in
strength ("Join us, join us, join us"). He's got rhythm.

The Rhythm Section

Avoiding inappropriate rhythms is easy enough. Only the
best writers, however, can go a step further and use
rhythm to make their meaning more meaningful. That
takes a good ear and plenty of practice. If you'd like to try,
listen to what you read, and learn from it. The writers you

admire probably use rhythm in ways you've never noticed; look up favorite passages and start listening.

Here's a sampling to get you started, from writers who use rhythm so well that it becomes part of the action. The first is from James Baldwin's *Go Tell It on the Mountain*. Listen to the biblical cadences in this rising storm of words:

"The morning of that day, as Gabriel rose and started out to work, the sky was low and nearly black and the air too thick to breathe. Late in the afternoon the wind rose, the skies opened, and the rain came. The rain came down as though once more in Heaven the Lord had been persuaded of the good uses of a flood. It drove before it the bowed wanderer, clapped children into houses, licked with fearful anger against the high, strong wall, and the wall of the lean-to, and the wall of the cabin, beat against the bark and the leaves of trees, trampled the broad grass, and broke the neck of the flower."

The passage owes its stately tread not just to the beat of the syllables, but also to repetition (*rose, rain, wall*) and to its forceful verbs (*drove, clapped, licked, beat, trampled, broke*).

Some mystery writers are wizards at using rhythm to convey fear and suspense. The rhythm in this passage from Elmore Leonard's *Glitz* underscores the confusion of a desperate fight scene:

"And Vincent closed and opened his eyes, saw her juggle the gun and drop it as Teddy slammed into him and Teddy's gun went off between them into the grocery sack of bottles, went off again and went off again, the bottles gone now as Vincent tried to grab hold of Teddy clinging to him and put him down, step on his gun. But something was wrong."

Nonfiction can be equally suspenseful. Barry Lopez, in *Arctic Dreams*, follows a long sentence with several short ones to convey the thrill he feels as he senses the presence of a group of narwhals, then the letdown when he misses a chance to see the elusive unicorns of the deep:

"I strained to see them, to spot the vapor of their breath, a warm mist against the soft horizon, or the white tip of a tusk breaking the surface of the water, a dark pattern that retained its shape against the dark, shifting patterns of the water. Somewhere out there in the ice fragments. Gone. Gone now."

Joseph Mitchell raised journalism to art in his profile of Joe Gould, a wandering Greenwich Village eccentric. In this passage, which you can find in Mitchell's book *Up in the Old Hotel*, the peripatetic rhythms are as circuitous as a typical day in Gould's life:

"I would see him sitting scribbling at a table in the Jackson Square branch of the Public Library, or I would see him filling his fountain pen in the main Village post office—the one on Tenth Street—or I would see him sitting among the young mothers and the old alcoholics in the sooty, pigeony, crumb-besprinkled, newspaper-bestrewn, privet-choked, coffin-shaped little park at Sheridan Square."

Note how the "I would see him" refrain and the *-ing* word ending reappear at intervals, just like Joe Gould. Then there's that loopy stream of adjectives at the end, as cranky and off-beat as Joe himself.

In her novel *Their Eyes Were Watching God*, Zora Neale Hurston invokes rhythms that re-create what's happening on the pages. Here she helps us hear as well as see the tossing of dice, the shuffling of cards:

"All the rest of the week Tea Cake was busy practicing up on his dice. He would flip them on the bare floor, on the rug and on the bed. He'd squat and throw, sit in a chair and throw and stand and throw. . . . Then he'd take his deck of cards and shuffle and cut, shuffle and cut and deal out and then examine each hand carefully, and do it again."

You can almost dance to some authors' rhythms, and what better way to write about dance than to imitate the rhythm of the movement? D. H. Lawrence, in an evocative essay called "The Dance of the Sprouting Corn," describes a Pueblo Indian ritual:

"Thud—thud—thud—thud—thud! goes the drum, heavily the men hop and hop and hop, sway, sway, sway, sway go the little branches of green pine. . . . The men are naked to the waist, and ruddy-golden, and in the rhythmic, hopping leap of the dance their breasts shake downwards, as the strong, heavy body comes down, down, down, down, in the downward plunge of the dance."

In much the same way, the sportswriter Red Smith used words to convey the rhythms of the boxing ring. This is from his column about the historic 1964 Sonny Liston–Cassius Clay match:

"Dancing, running, jabbing, ducking, stopping now and then to pepper the champion's head with potshots in swift combinations, he had won the first, third, and fourth rounds and opened an angry cut under Liston's left eye."

Some of the most rhythmic writing anywhere can be found in the Bible. Here's a passage from the Song of Solomon, in the King James Version:

"My beloved spake, and said unto me, Rise up, my love, my fair one, and come away. For, lo, the winter is past, the rain is over and gone; the flowers appear on the earth; the time of the singing of birds is come; and the voice of the turtle is heard in our land."

Rhythm doesn't get much better. But then, we expect rhythm in biblical writing. We don't expect to find it in writing on, let's say, mathematics. Unexpected pleasures are the sweetest. In their book *The Reader over Your Shoulder*, Robert Graves and Alan Hodge tell a story about a mathematical work that included this sentence:

"It may at first sight seem unlikely that the pull of gravity will depress the center of a light cord, held horizontally at a high lateral tension; and yet no force, however great, can stretch a cord, however fine, into a horizontal line that shall be absolutely straight."

Years after the work was published, a careful reader discovered the perfect little rhymed poem hidden in the second half of the sentence. Someone was listening.

To judge the cadences of your own writing, speak the lines aloud, or at least recite them in your head. For comparison, think of some familiar rhythms. If you ride, think of a horse's gaits: walk, trot, canter, gallop. If you're musical, use your toe or an imaginary baton to mark the tempo: adagio, andante, allegro, presto. Think of an oncoming train, the waves of the sea, wheels on a cobblestone street.

If speaking your own words makes you feel silly, rest assured that you're not the first to do it. Flaubert went outdoors and tested his phrases by shouting them from his terrace. C. K. Scott Moncrieff, the translator of Proust, held forth out on the moors. When words don't sound right, something's wrong. Next time, don't just write. Listen.

25

The Human Comedy

WHAT'S SO FUNNY?

This is probably my favorite joke in the whole world: A horse walks into a bar. The bartender says, "Hey, buddy, why the long face?"

Well, it works for me. I first heard it about ten years ago from a colleague at the *New York Times Book Review*, where the level of humor is extremely elevated. I was useless for the rest of the day. You'd think I'd be sick of the joke by now, but it still reduces me to Jell-O.

I like to think of myself as a woman of the world, a person of some sophistication. Then what do I see in such a corny joke? I've been giving this some thought, and I have a few conclusions.

First, I like jokes that begin with animals walking into bars: ducks, parrots, French poodles, kangaroos, and so on. Another joke I like starts with a duck walking into a hardware store. Heard it from the same guy, in fact.* Second, I like the juxtaposition of the ridiculous and the routine. Third, I like plays on words. And finally, I like a joke I can remember.

Now you know how to make me laugh. How do you make your readers laugh?

While no piece of writing is funny to everyone, it's safe to say that some things are inherently humorous. Penguins are funnier than seagulls. A rutabaga is funnier than a carrot, and a nose job is funnier than an appendectomy. Three clergymen in a lifeboat are funnier than one in a canoe. A jock strap sounds funnier than an athletic supporter, and a truss is funnier still (unless you're the guy who needs one). We know this instinctively, even if we've never stopped to wonder why.

It's certainly more fun to laugh at humor than to analyze it. But putting comedy on the couch can make your own writing funnier. Read humorous writing and look for a method to the madness. Is it parody? Ridicule? Gross exaggeration? Slapstick? Absurd juxtaposition? Incongruous situations? Great timing? Euphemism gone mad? Pomposity deflated?

Look for opportunities to use humor. An amusing anecdote at the beginning of a long essay, for instance, might draw readers in and make it seem less formidable. A few well-placed laughs along the way could provide comic

---

*If you must know, see the appendix.

relief. And a light note at the end might be precisely what it takes to drive home your point and make it stick. No kidding.

Remember that most writers aren't relentlessly funny from beginning to end, and they don't have to be. A pinch of humor that works is better than a potful that doesn't. For most of us humor is merely seasoning; it's not the whole dish. Some of the following examples are from humorists and some from writers who use only a strategic giggle here or there. Enjoy them.

Comic Relief

We've all had to suffer through the boring lecture or sermon or sales pitch that never seems to stop. You know the kind. Just as you think the speaker is coming to the end, you find he's only reached the small intestine.

Remember your sufferings next time you have to write something packed with information. Have mercy on your readers. So what if they don't expect to be entertained? Surprise them. See how the astronomer Fred Hoyle, in his book *The Nature of the Universe,* lightens up what could have been a weighty discussion of the immensity of space:

"One of the questions we shall have to consider later is what lies beyond the range of our most powerful instruments. But even within the range of observation there are about 100,000,000 galaxies. With upward of 1,000,000 planetary systems per galaxy the combined total for the parts of the Universe that we can see comes out at more than a hundred million million. I find myself wondering whether somewhere among them there is a cricket team that could beat the Australians."

When you have to rattle off a list of numbers, facts, projections, or whatever, give your audience a break. Put something light at the end of the tunnel.

The Last Laugh

I don't find insects amusing. And scientific writing isn't usually a lot of laughs. Still, a good writer can find humor in almost anything. I couldn't help smiling at this passage about ants, from Lewis Thomas's *The Lives of a Cell*.

"Ants are so much like human beings as to be an embarrassment. They farm fungi, raise aphids as livestock, launch armies into wars, use chemical sprays to alarm and confuse enemies, capture slaves. The families of weaver ants engage in child labor, holding their larvae like shuttles to spin out the thread that sews the leaves together for their fungus gardens. They exchange information ceaselessly. They do everything but watch television."

Yes, it's funny that ants are so much like us at our worst, with their armies, chemical weapons, slavery, and child labor. But what makes the paragraph work is its timing: The best line is saved for last. When you write, be sure you haven't buried a punch line.

Hyper Ventilation

In humor, the next best thing to understatement is overstatement. Or maybe it's the other way around. Either way, I can't exaggerate the place of exaggeration in funny writing. So I'll let P. G. Wodehouse do it for me. In this excerpt from *Right Ho, Jeeves*, Bertie Wooster describes drinking his man Jeeves's famous pick-me-up, a remarkably effective morning-after concoction:

"For perhaps the split part of a second nothing happens. It is as though all Nature waited breathless. Then, suddenly, it is as if the Last Trump had sounded and Judgement Day set in with unusual severity.

"Bonfires burst out in all parts of the frame. The abdomen becomes heavily charged with molten lava. A great wind seems to blow through the world, and the subject is aware of something resembling a steam hammer striking the back of the head. During this phase, the ears ring loudly, the eyeballs rotate and there is a tingling about the brow.

"And then, just as you are feeling that you ought to ring up your lawyer and see that your affairs are in order before it is too late, the whole situation seems to clarify. The wind drops. The ears cease to ring. Birds twitter. Brass bands start playing. The sun comes up over the horizon with a jerk.

"And a moment later all you are conscious of is a great peace."

Like Wodehouse, you can make excess a virtue. Pile it on. Use embellishment for its own sake. Sometimes too much is just enough.

A Little off the Top

The mighty, it seems, were meant to fall. When this happens in Greek drama, the mighty one is brought down by some tragic flaw. When it happens in comedy, he trips over an ottoman or slips on a banana peel or gets a pie in the face. We love to laugh at the evil figure cut down to size, the pompous one humbled, the bully put in his place.

In his short story "The Schmeed Memoirs," Woody Allen whittles down some oversized villains. The narrator is a barber reminiscing about his celebrity clients:

"In the spring of 1940, a large Mercedes pulled up in front of my barbershop at 127 Koenigstrasse, and Hitler walked in. 'I just want a light trim,' he said, 'and don't take too much off the top.' I explained to him there would be a brief wait because von Ribbentrop was ahead of him. Hitler said he was in a rush and asked Ribbentrop if he could be taken next, but Ribbentrop insisted it would look bad for the Foreign Office if he were passed over. Hitler thereupon made a quick phone call, and Ribbentrop was immediately transferred to the Afrika Korps, and Hitler got his haircut. This sort of rivalry went on all the time. Once, Göring had Heydrich detained by the police on false pretenses, so that he could get the chair by the window. Göring was a dissolute and often wanted to sit on the hobbyhorse to get his haircuts."

Monsters can make us shudder or they can make us laugh. If laughter is what you're after, the next time you peer into the jaws of evil don't forget to examine the bridgework.

Uneasy Street

Have you ever been in an awkward situation, the kind that makes you squirm even in retrospect? This same predicament might be hilarious to somebody else. Sure, you get hives when you think about the time you were stuck with your ex in an elevator for three hours. But it might make a great anecdote to liven up that speech you have to give at the divorce lawyers' conference next week.

Damon Runyon was a master at finding humor in uncomfortable situations. In his short story "Butch Minds the Baby," a former safecracker is watching Junior while his wife is out for the evening. As he fans the sleeping baby, three former associates drop by and ask him to come out of retirement and take on one last job. Butch agrees, but there's a catch: "I dast not leave little John Ignatius Junior for a minute." So the baby comes along on the heist. (They cut him in for five percent.) Let's listen to the narrator, who's "more nervous than somewhat," as he describes the artist at work:

"He starts drilling into the safe around the combination lock, working very fast and very quiet, when all of a sudden what happens but John Ignatius Junior sits up on the blanket and lets out a squall. Naturally this is most disquieting to me, and personally I am in favor of beaning John Ignatius Junior with something to make him keep still, because I am nervous enough as it is. But the squalling does not seem to bother Big Butch. He lays down his tools and picks up John Ignatius Junior and starts whispering, 'There, there, there, my itty oddleums. Da-dad is here.'"

The safe is forgotten as Butch gets out the Sterno and warms a bottle. Later, the job completed, somebody trips an alarm, and soon the streets are full of police. But little John Ignatius Junior saves the day. Butch walks away a free man, since no cop in his right mind would suspect a party carrying a baby.

As you cast about for humorous subjects to lighten that op-ed piece or alumni newsletter or address to the Odd Fellows, don't overlook the sticky situation. That fine mess you got yourself into may be a million laughs—to somebody else.

Through the Magnifying Glass

Let's admit it. We get most of our laughs at the other guy's expense. You can make anyone or anything look ridiculous by picking out a tiny flaw and magnifying it out of all proportion. Unfair, you say? So what else is new?

Mark Twain didn't much care for James Fenimore Cooper, the author of those adventure novels about Indians and woodsmen. In what must be one of the funniest book reviews ever written, Twain mercilessly dissects some of Cooper's sillier literary techniques:

"A favorite one was to make a moccasined person tread in the tracks of the moccasined enemy, and thus hide his own trail. Cooper wore out barrels and barrels of moccasins in working that trick. Another stage-property that he pulled out of his box pretty frequently was his broken twig. He prized his broken twig above all the rest of his effects, and worked it the hardest. It is a restful chapter in any book of his when somebody doesn't step on a dry twig and alarm all the reds and whites for two hundred yards around. Every time a Cooper person is in peril, and absolute silence is worth four dollars a minute, he is sure to step on a dry twig. There may be a hundred handier things to step on, but that wouldn't satisfy Cooper. Cooper requires him to turn out and find a dry twig; and if he can't do it, go and borrow one."

Think of that dry twig when you next set out to skewer something. By exaggerating one or two weaknesses, you can puncture an inflated ego or expose the ridiculous. Or you can be just plain ornery.

Tickled to Death

Now and then euphemisms come in handy. They let you tell a caller that your hubby is indisposed, not that he's sitting on the loo. (Come to think of it, *loo* is a euphemism, too.) But what's useful in small doses can be a dandy comic technique when taken to extremes.

I know of no better example of euphemism run amok than the famous dead-parrot sketch written by John Cleese and Graham Chapman for television's Monty Python troupe and embellished over the years. We'll join the conversation as a customer returns to a pet shop to complain about a recent purchase:

"He's bleedin' demised! He's passed on! This parrot is no more! He has ceased to be! He's expired and gone to meet his maker! He's a stiff! Bereft of life, he rests in peace! If you hadn't nailed him to the perch he'd be pushing up the daisies! His metabolic processes are now history! He's off the twig! He's kicked the bucket, he's shuffled off his mortal coil, rung down the curtain and joined the bleedin' choir invisible! This is an ex-parrot!"

We don't normally find death funny. In fact, death makes us so uncomfortable that we talk about it in euphemisms. But taken to ridiculous lengths, the forbidden subject itself becomes ridiculous. If you want to write humorously about sex or money or the Grim Reaper or some other delicate matter, get out your thesaurus and collect every outrageous euphemism you can find.

Theater of the Absurd

Remember Wile E. Coyote, the inept villain in the Road Runner cartoons? His intricate schemes always went awry. Bombs exploded prematurely in his face; giant rubber bands hurled him into boulders; jet-propelled skates shot him through billboards, where he left behind a hole in the shape of his silhouette. Imagine if he had sued the manufacturer of all those faulty products. Ian Frazier imagined it, and the result is his short story "Coyote v. Acme." Let's listen in as the plaintiff's attorney delivers his opening statement in the United States District Court for the Southwestern District, Tempe, Arizona:

"Mr. Coyote states that on December 13th he reccived of Defendant via parcel post one Acme Rocket Sled. The intention of Mr. Coyote was to use the Rocket Sled to aid him in pursuit of his prey. Upon receipt of the Rocket Sled Mr. Coyote removed it from its wooden shipping crate and, sighting his prey in the distance, activated the ignition. As Mr. Coyote gripped the handlebars, the Rocket Sled accelerated with such sudden and precipitate force as to stretch Mr. Coyote's forelimbs to a length of fifty feet. Subsequently, the rest of Mr. Coyote's body shot forward with a violent jolt, causing severe strain to his back and neck and placing him unexpectedly astride the Rocket Sled."

What follows is a litany of mishaps involving various products and a request for damages in the amount of $38,750,000 against the Acme Company, its directors, officers, shareholders, successors, and assigns.

What's so funny? In a word, it's absurd. How often do we see a cartoon character in a real court of law, his improbable bodily injuries described in deadpan medical terminology?

You can use this technique, too. Let your imagination off the leash. Be incongruous. And incongruouser and incongruouser. Imagine the dust bunnies under your bed coming to life. Dr. Ruth as a marriage counselor at the court of Henry VIII. Your toaster oven plotting to short-circuit the microwave. A couple of newborns in a hospital nursery scheming to swap parents.

As for Mr. Coyote, I think he has a pretty good case.

At Wits' End

If you want to write humor, read humor. There are many more ways to be funny than the few I've talked about. Use those that seem most natural to you, and never strain to get a laugh.

If you have doubts about whether something's funny, play it straight. Nothing is worse than a lame joke. And if you're not sure humor is appropriate, it probably isn't. What leaves you rolling on the floor might not go over so well with Aunt Mabel. As Mel Brooks put it: "Tragedy is when I cut my finger. Comedy is when you fall into an open manhole and die."

egug...
jghrtgerfdtsyhejuogehtrysfertdgwrsteyhfushkey
dhtjncge...hiduwournhrsgeyifkdleystqnnaqmmxusdn
pjste...teujnflksmcdafewdurheksjfredhulisfd
lryusfetrdgshuwyrtghsyeturheydfgj
hrtegsfdytjhrjuktjfgersfegydthmburfdgsyegfhsuyef

I Second That Emotion

ONCE MORE, WITH FEELING

Of course you care. You feel things deeply. I do, too. But we can write about feelings without letting feelings run the show. We don't have to hit readers over the head to get across fear, sorrow, love, pity, jealousy, greed, and other powerful emotions. Writing is more moving when it leaves something to the imagination.

Take Alfred Hitchcock's *Psycho*. It's one of the scariest of all scary movies. Why? Because it's one of the least bloody. Hitchcock forces us to imagine the most frightening parts, and nothing on the big screen could be as frightening as the workings of a frightened mind.

Good writers make the reader's imagination work for them. Say you want to describe an avaricious corporate biggie. You could come right out with it: "He's a greedy SOB." Or you could quote the SOB himself—"The hell with an eighty-five percent market share, I want it all!"—and let the reader figure it out.

Sometimes it's not what you put in that stays with the reader—it's what you leave out. If you're writing a research paper that has a particularly ominous conclusion, you don't have to tell readers how ominous it is. Let the research speak for itself.

Think of the writing that moves you the most. I'll bet the writer holds something back, something you have to fill in yourself. Good writing is not a spectator sport; both the writer and the reader participate. Whenever I reread something that's affected me deeply, I'm surprised at how much of what I remember is my contribution.

Now I'll show you some writing that conveys powerful emotion without overwrought language. Instead, readers are drawn in with evocative details and invited to fill in the blanks.

Drop by Drop

Primo Levi survived the Holocaust but never left its horrors behind. In this passage from *Survival in Auschwitz*, he describes his arrival at the concentration camp. Freezing, hungry, and desperately thirsty after four days in a cattle car, Levi and his fellow prisoners are put in a cold room where drops of putrid water fall from a faucet:

"A huge, empty room: we are tired, standing on our

feet, with a tap which drips while we cannot drink the water, and we wait for something which will certainly be terrible, and nothing happens and nothing continues to happen. What can one think about? One cannot think any more, it is like being already dead. Someone sits down on the ground. The time passes drop by drop."

With one small detail—the relentless drip of the tap—Levi sums up the fear and dread of waiting for an unknown terror.

Body Language

Jealousy is a difficult emotion to describe, particularly in first-person writing. A mere "Boy, was I jealous!" doesn't cut the mustard. In this passage from her novel *A Thousand Acres*, Jane Smiley portrays jealousy without using the word. The narrator, Ginny, who has nursed her sister through an illness, learns that Rose has stolen her lover. She thinks of the two familiar bodies, now secretly sharing an intimacy that each once shared with her:

"And so, here, at last, was Rose, all that bone and flesh, right next to, right in the same bed with, Jess Clark. If I remembered hard enough I could smell her odor, feel the exact dry quality of her skin, smell and feel her the way he did during those mysterious times when I wasn't around. I could smell and feel and hear and see him, too, with a force unmatched since the first few days after we had sex. . . . Every time I could not actually see one or the other of them, I had a visceral conviction that they were together."

Amazing, isn't it? A few intimate details can conjure

up the ravenous green-eyed monster. Technicolor and Surround sound are not required.

The Wing of Madness

William Styron has described his terrifying descent into depression as an overwhelming horror that the feeble word *depression* only makes a mockery of. But in his memoir *Darkness Visible* he does something better than merely describe this torment; he helps the reader see it through the eyes of a sufferer. In this passage, he suddenly realizes how ill he is:

"One bright day on a walk through the woods with my dog I heard a flock of Canada geese honking high above the trees ablaze with foliage; ordinarily a sight and sound that would have exhilarated me, the flight of birds caused me to stop, riveted with fear, and I stood stranded there, helpless, shivering, aware for the first time that I had been stricken by no mere pangs of withdrawal but by a serious illness whose name and actuality I was able finally to acknowledge. Going home, I couldn't rid my mind of the line of Baudelaire's, dredged up from the distant past, that for several days had been skittering around at the edge of my consciousness: 'I have felt the wind of the wing of madness.'"

Much later, as Styron's depression begins to lift, another wild bird appears, but this one is a sign of hope: "Although I was still shaky I knew I had emerged into light. I felt myself no longer a husk but a body with some of the body's sweet juices stirring again. I had my first dream in many months, confused but to this day imperishable, with a flute in it somewhere, and a wild goose, and a dancing girl."

Styron doesn't just tell us the madness is loosening its grip. He shows us how he knows.

Crows in a Graveyard

Frank McCourt, in *Angela's Ashes*, writes about the anger he felt as a child when a little brother died senselessly. He doesn't say he was angry, but who can doubt it after reading this bleak burial passage?

"I did not like the jackdaws that perched on trees and gravestones and I did not want to leave Oliver with them. I threw a rock at a jackdaw that waddled over toward Oliver's grave. Dad said I shouldn't throw rocks at jackdaws, they might be somebody's soul. I didn't know what a soul was but I didn't ask him because I didn't care. Oliver was dead and I hated jackdaws. I'd be a man someday and I'd come back with a bag of rocks and I'd leave the graveyard littered with dead jackdaws."

As young Frank strikes out at the crows in the cemetery, we can feel his rage over Oliver's death. You might remember that when you write about strong feelings. Give just enough detail to summon up the emotion. The readers will do the rest themselves.

Love Potions

One day I idly picked up Jane Austen's *Emma* and turned to my favorite scene. It's the ninth inning, and Mr. Knightley, the man Emma has loved for years without realizing it, declares his love for her. The two of them, alone in a garden, are overcome with emotion.

I'd remembered Emma's response as passionate and tumultuous, a three-hanky job. But wait a minute. Where's the moving declaration of love? This is all that Austen tells us about Emma's reply: "What did she say? Just what she ought, of course. A lady always does."

It's a wonderful scene, but what makes it wonderful is what's left out. Without realizing it, we provide the missing pieces as we read. We use our imaginations. And later we remember that scene as being more impassioned than it actually is. Austen does more without words than most writers do with them.

A Glance Is Enough

For expressing feelings, nothing beats simple, honest writing. One small detail, such as a shoe washed up on a beach, can be more tragic than a graphic description of a drowning victim's body. A simple sentence about a honeymoon cottage with its curtains drawn for days on end can say more about passion than a catalog of sexual particulars.

Never underestimate the power of understatement. Wield a fine brush, not a trowel. You can move readers without resorting to corny clichés, icky sentiment, and heavy-handed goop.

"When there are no words," Flaubert wrote, "a glance is enough."

The Importance of Being Honest

LEVELING WITH THE READER

How often do we read things we don't believe, by authors who don't believe them either? I'm not talking about stretching the truth with exaggerations like "One size fits all" or "Easy to assemble." And I don't mean occasional white lies, the harmless fibs everyone uses now and then: "Wish you were here" or "It's just what I wanted!" I'm talking about those little gray lies we read all the time, the ones sneaky writers use to say something without really saying it.

"This isn't aimed at you personally," your supervisor writes in a negative evaluation. (Oh yes it is.)

"I don't mean to criticize," a neighbor says in a note about the wildflower meadow you've decided to grow instead of a lawn. (Oh yes she does.)

"I'm not a demanding person," your father-in-law writes, then proceeds to tell you exactly how he'd like his breakfast prepared when he comes to visit. (Oh yes he is.)

That type of dishonest writing doesn't fool anybody. We know it's not true, the writers know it's not true, and we know they know we know. So why the empty disclaimers? Let's look at a few of them and find out.

Cowardly Lying

Many writers lie with the best of intentions. They have bad news to deliver, so they try to soften the blow. Imagine you're a violin teacher, writing a six-month review of little Herschel's progress. How do you tell his folks it's hopeless because Herschel can't play in tune?

You could take the spineless way out: *I won't say that Herschel is entirely without talent for the violin, but it may not be in his best interest to continue.*

Or you could tell the truth, but tactfully: *The violin is not Herschel's instrument because he has a poor sense of pitch. But he enjoys music and has good rhythm, so why not let him try the drums?*

A lie doesn't really soften a blow. It's often kinder to tell the truth, especially if there's some good in it.

The Sneak Charmer

A weaselly writer can always find a way to sneak in an opinion without taking responsibility for it. The most common method, the back-door denial, has become familiar enough that we take it for granted. How many times have you read statements like these?

No one's suggesting war is a good thing. (Translation: It has its points.)

Not all performance artists are weird. (Just most of them.)

Not every pit bull is a killer. (Show me one that isn't.)

Lawyers don't always have their hands in our pockets. (They have to eat sometime.)

I wouldn't say teenagers are difficult. (They're hell on earth.)

Patent-leather pumps are not unattractive. (I wouldn't be caught dead in them.)

Her last production wasn't a total flop. (It bombed.)

Writers play this game when they don't have the courage to be honest.

I've heard of a college professor who didn't want to offend mediocre job applicants asking for letters of recommendation. He was reluctant to lie, but he didn't want to tell the truth, either, so he prepared a few stock comments that could be read in two ways: "I would urge you to waste no time in making this candidate an offer of employment. . . . In my opinion, you will be very fortunate to get this person to work for you. . . . I most enthusiastically recommend this candidate with no qualifications whatsoever."

The One That Got Away

Everyone exaggerates from time to time, and we accept that as part of being human. We don't take fish stories seriously, for example, unless the fish is in evidence. We also don't mind an exaggeration or two in humorous writing, like the yo-yo dieter's lament that her butt is as big as a Buick.

But if you want to be believed, go easy on the hyperbole. If readers think you're stretching a point here or there, even a minor one, they might suspect everything you write. Suppose you're arguing against the construction of a car wash on your street. You make a good case, based on an engineering report about potential waterpressure and drainage problems. You'd only weaken your petition to the planning commission by throwing in wild speculation about thousands of cars driving through every hour, honking noisily, and generally disturbing the peace.

Be honest. Trust the bare facts (or the bare events, if you're writing fiction). Things are amazing enough as they are. The padding will make what's underneath look suspicious.

Scare Tactics

Readers know when you're leveling with them and when you're not. You may grab their attention the first time you raise an alarm for no good reason. But it won't work the second time. A parents' group, for instance, would stir up more skepticism than support by citing unfounded predictions that four out of five kids who play video games will end up in prison.

A writer depends on the trust of readers. A good way

to lose it is to sound a false alarm. I make it a rule never to cry wolf unless there are at least three of them at the door.

Writing Is Believing

The way to make readers believe what you write is to write only what you believe. This is true for fiction, too. It won't be believable if the author doesn't believe in it.

In *The Human Comedy*, Balzac created a doctor named Bianchon. It's said that years later, when he was on his deathbed, Balzac cried: "Send for Bianchon. Bianchon will save me." Now that's believing in what you write.

28

Once around the Block

WHAT TO DO WHEN YOU'RE STUCK

Stuck, are you? Everybody is, now and then. Writer's block is not a character flaw, and it's not permanent, or at least not usually. Most writers, including some of the best, have gotten stuck but have survived to write again. The question isn't whether you'll get back to your writing, but when—and how much time you'll waste in the interim.

Don't panic just yet. You may not be as stuck as you think. There's stuck, and then there's *stuck*. Don't lose sight of the progress you've made. A minor hurdle can seem mountainous if you think you're getting nowhere. Take another look at the signs of progress described in chapter 5.

Now, in the interest of making your pause a brief one, let's get on with it.

Short-Term Therapy

Writer's block is like the flu. Everybody has a favorite cure. What works for one person may not work for another, and what works today may not work tomorrow. If your case is a mild one, here are some folk remedies you might try.

- Take a shower. It's relaxing, and everybody thinks in the shower. If you don't get ideas there, you're hopeless.
- Go for a walk. Once around the block can't hurt. Suck in some fresh air, get the red corpuscles moving, give those tired gray cells a break.
- Eat something. Nobody writes well on an empty stomach. Don't stuff yourself, though, or you'll write like a slug.
- Read something. For a few minutes of R&R, try a quick shot of a writer you like—a page or two of Fran Lebowitz, or Wordsworth, or Stephen Hawking, or Barbara Pym. But make it a mini-vacation, not an extended stay.
- Change clothes. You may be itchy or pinched, too warm or too cold. Put on something more comfortable. And don't try to write in spandex. You may cut off circulation to the brain.

I know what you're thinking. Hmmm, those remedies sound like fun. But I'm way ahead of you. If you take ten or fifteen minutes to eat a BLT, add another ten or fifteen minutes to your writing session.

Detour Ahead

When you're driving in the country and come to a washed-out bridge, you don't park by the side of the road until it's repaired. You go around.

Writers hit washed-out bridges, too. They know where they're going, but they can't see how to get there from here. Maybe a passage seems impossible to write, a crucial piece of information is somewhere out in the ozone, or the perfect word is just out of reach. Some writers doggedly keep at it until they solve the problem. Some freeze up, chewing their nails and accomplishing nothing as they stare into the abyss. And some sensible souls detour around the obstacle, then come back to it later with a fresh perspective.

Guess which course I recommend.

Imagine you're humming merrily along on a writing project, perhaps an article for a dog magazine on house-training in the city, when you come to what seems an insurmountable problem: How do you rush a puppy to the street when you live on the forty-ninth floor of a high-rise building? You stop to think. You think some more. The longer you stare at the problem, the larger it looms. Sweat appears on your upper lip. How much time is this going to cost? Hours, days, weeks? Panic sets in. Before you know it, you're blocked but good.

My advice is to skirt the problem before you become catatonic. I know of a novelist who was on the brink of a full-blown case of writer's block. His publisher was breathing down his neck, and he couldn't figure out how to get his villain from chapter 11 to chapter 13, the pivotal point in the story. No, he didn't sit there like a zombie while the clock slowly ticked. Instead, he pretended he'd solved the problem. He typed "Chapter 12" at the top of a page, followed by a long chunk of gibberish, then went on with chapter 13 and "finished" the book. When he went back to the problem with a fresh eye, the solution seemed obvious.

So when an intimidating obstacle threatens to derail your history paper or sales pitch, take a detour, especially if you're on a tight deadline and can't afford the delay. But don't cook up excuses to leave behind a lot of unfinished business. Skip over a problem only if it is stopping you dead. It's not a good idea to bypass something that's not a real threat, something you can handle without breaking stride.

A note of caution: This trick works only if you know where you're going. If you don't, jumping ahead can backfire. What if you return to the article on house-training and decide that the only solution is to get a cat? Now you're really in a pickle.

Mission Impossible

When I bog down, it's often because I'm trying to solve the wrong problem. After wasting days at a time on a single paragraph, I discover that it doesn't work because (surprise!) it's unworkable. I may be trying to prove a controversial point, make a difficult case, or justify a startling conclusion. In the end, it turns out that the point can't be proved, or the case can't be made, or the conclusion isn't justified.

Perhaps you're writing a paper on the history of photography. You have a hunch that peeping-Tom arrests rose sharply after the development of the telephoto lens, and you'd like to toss that in as a sidelight. But you can't prove it. Each avenue of research is a dead end. Your progress comes to a halt. You begin to doubt yourself, and writer's block sets in.

Hold on there. Maybe the problem isn't you but the point you're trying to make. Your hunch may not be right, after all. Drop it and get on with your paper.

Then again, your hunch may be correct. But if the paper is due tomorrow and you don't have time to do the necessary research, drop that point anyway. Don't blow your project by going off on an impossible mission.

Fuel Crisis

Once in a while you'll poop out simply because you've run out of material to work with. If you're lucky, what you need is there in your notes and you've just forgotten about it. Return to your notes. A fresh look at them might give you some ideas and get you going again.

Or perhaps you started writing too soon, and you didn't gather enough material in the first place. You'll need to gather more, to learn more about your subject. Don't stop writing completely while you visit the library or navigate cyberspace, though. Go back and forth between writing and researching so you don't stall. Once your engine cools off, it's hard to get it started again.

The Wrong Track

Have you ever had driving directions that you dutifully followed—to the middle of nowhere? When you stubbornly follow a writing idea that's going nowhere, that's exactly where you'll end up. If you're stalled and nothing else works, consider the possibility that you need a new approach. Look at the subject from a different angle.

Say you're writing a sales brochure for a new retirement community. You start by emphasizing the wonderful on-site medical care, including a twelve-bed clinic with three nurses and a full-time doctor. The more you discuss how ideal the place is for geezers on their last legs, the grimmer it sounds. You wanted to make it appear lively and fun, not like the last stop before the cemetery. Now you're stuck because there's no graceful way to get to the goodies. So scratch the medical approach. Think healthy and active instead of sick. Build your brochure around entertainment and recreation. Emphasize the golf course, the pool, the tennis courts, and the busy social calendar. Yes, mention the terrific medical care, but only in passing.

Fear Itself

In high school, at the excruciatingly self-conscious age of fifteen, I had to give a speech before the Lions Club. My hands shook at the typewriter as I wrote it. I'd never met a Lion, let alone a den full of them. How that speech was written I'll never know.

When I stood up to deliver it, though, I was fine. The Lions, it turned out, were pussycats. As soon as I saw them, so friendly and encouraging, I relaxed.

Sometimes writer's block is simply fear of the un-known: the audience. When you can't picture your read-ers, it's hard to write with confidence. And if you imagine the worst—a pack of snarling critics, just waiting to tear you to pieces—you'll be paralyzed. You'll be your own worst critic, picking apart every word and phrase. And fearful or self-conscious writing is stilted writing.

I've noticed that little children write as they speak—naturally. They haven't yet learned the fear of writing. Try to remember how you felt before the self-consciousness set in. Picture a friendly audience, one that's interested in what you have to say and that wants to believe you. Even when that's not the case, and the readers hate your guts, pretend they're on your side. The writing will be easier and—who knows?—you may win them over.

Playing with Blocks

You can have writer's block and never know it. You may think you're working on a project when in fact you're putting off the writing.

Some people spend years researching histories or memoirs or Ph.D. theses that are never written. They have more than enough material early on, but somehow can't make themselves sit down and write. They seem busy and create the illusion that they're making progress, but the endless research eventually becomes an excuse not to write.

You can avoid this trap. Set aside a specific amount of time for writing—and *only* writing. Don't use that time for research. If you find you need to do additional re-search, do it during some other part of the day.

Imagine you're writing an essay on gun control. Along the way, you get an idea. Maybe crime in the Old West shot up when the revolver was introduced. But this is your writing time, pal. You don't want to get mired in research just now. Instead of stopping work to go to the library and hit the books (or maybe the CD-ROM's), skip over the missing part and move on. Put in a few dummy sentences to hold the fort:

In 18XX, as law enforcement in the West was blah blah blah quack quack quack yadda yadda yadda, Samuel Colt invented the revolver. In the next XX decades, crime in frontier towns yackety-yack yackety-yack, with the result that blah blah blah blah blah.

Research isn't the only thing that can keep you from writing. Any distraction will do in a squeeze. If you've set aside two hours each morning for a week to work on a project, keep to your schedule. Get your teeth cleaned or your hair cut or your car lubed in the afternoon. There's always something. The habitual excuse is only writer's block in disguise.

Now get back to work.

29

Debt before Dishonor

HOW AND WHAT TO BORROW

I've long envied a friend of mine for the way she dresses. She's always beautifully put together, even in jeans. Give her a black T-shirt and a scarf and she can go anywhere. I remember studying her once at a party, wondering how she did it. She was elegance itself, wearing—of all things—a gray silk kimono and black high-top sneakers.

I felt like a schlub. "How can I not have a gray silk kimono and black high-tops?" I thought.

I'm a slow learner, you see. It took me a while to realize that the things she wore didn't matter. What mattered was why she chose them. I didn't need her kimono. I needed to learn what she knew about style.

I envy a lot of writers, too, but I don't steal what they've written. (There are laws about that sort of thing.) Instead I try to steal some of the tricks that make their writing so good. How? I thought you'd never ask.

Showstoppers

Suppose you have to cover a football game for your college newspaper and the outcome is a foregone conclusion. The game is a numbing bore, and there's not much to report other than the score. What to do? Why not look at what writers you admire have done in similar jams?

Red Smith, my favorite sportswriter, once went to a dog show where the defending champion—or "ch."— was considered a shoo-in. Rather than write a ho-hum column about the dog's inevitable victory, Smith sized up some of the handlers and judges:

"It is a scientific fact that the ladies tethered to the tiny toys are invariably the most magnificent members of the species. No exception was taken in this case; the smallest pooch noted was towing the largest handler, a celestial creature measuring seventeen and a half hands at the withers, deep of chest, with fine, sturdy pasterns. . . .

"The judge of the nonsporting group, a Dr. M. Ross Taylor, proved himself a ch. among chs. He was imperious; he was painstakingly studious; he was profoundly author-itative of mien. He had splendid conformation—broad shoulders, white hair, and an erect carriage—and was beautifully turned out in an ensemble of rich brown."

Now, try to apply Red Smith's example to your boring football game. Instead of writing a predictable account of a predictable game, you could turn the story on its head.

Look at the scene from a different perspective. A dull game may be good news for the hot dog and soda vendors. Ask a few busy concessionaires what they think makes a memorable day at the stadium. (Don't forget to include the score and a few details for the record. This is a sports story, after all.)

Borrowing from writers you like doesn't mean aping their work or their style. If you were writing about a dog show instead of a football game, you wouldn't want to size up the humans as Red Smith did. That's not plagiarism, but it smells a lot like it. If you were covering a beauty pageant, however, you might adapt his idea by describing the physical charms of the emcee and the judges. And you'd sleep with a clear conscience.

Crabby Ways

Barbara Kingsolver is another writer worth borrowing from. She has a knack for getting into a subject in an interesting way. Her essay "High Tide in Tucson" begins with a story about a hermit crab she accidentally brought home to Arizona. It was sleeping in a shell she found in the Bahamas, and awoke to find itself on her coffee table. Buster, as she called the crab, adapted to life in the desert but held on to the old, familiar rhythms. And so, it turns out, did she.

"When I was twenty-two, I donned the shell of a tiny yellow Renault and drove with all I owned from Kentucky to Tucson. . . . I'm here for good, it seems. And yet I never cease to long in my bones for what I left behind."

That longing is what Kingsolver's essay is all about.

She uses the uprooted crab and its crabby ways to sum up her own experience with uprootedness. "Yeah," you're thinking, "that's a neat trick, but what's in it for me?"

Perhaps you've been chosen to make a speech at the retirement dinner for the local head librarian. He's famous for anticipating readers' tastes, for knowing what they like before they do. In fact, he turned you on to your favorite author, P. G. Wodehouse. You could begin your tribute with an anecdote about Jeeves, the omniscient butler who anticipates Bertie Wooster's every whim. Then compare the Wodehouse character to the prescient librarian who led you to him. There's your crab!

Whine Not

I don't know about you, but I tend to tire of whiny writing. Not that writers don't have a right to feel sorry for themselves on occasion. I just don't want to read about it.

One reason I like Cynthia Heimel is that she manages to whimper and whine without actually whimpering and whining. She does it by laughing at herself. That's my kind of woman. Take her column about how hard it is to lose weight. Here, she's just met with the dietician and agreed to a regimen of salad and crackers:

"'You'll lose twenty pounds in a month,' she says.

"'I'm your girl,' I say.

"I go home and start the famous prediet ritual: Eating everything I can. Cheeseburgers. Fries. Mallomars. Quite a few Mallomars. I want to throw up."

The next morning, the diet begins: "Please, somebody feed me. I'm going to faint. I'm starving to death."

Again, what's to learn? A downer goes down easier with a little humor. If you're writing about a bad experience—something depressing or discouraging—lighten up. There's probably an element of humor in there somewhere.

Say you're the marketing manager for a toy manufacturer and you're writing a training booklet for new sales reps. You want to warn them about how demoralizing it is to walk into a toy store and try to wheedle shelf space for another board game. Rather than scare them with horror stories and failure rates, why not laugh at some of the mistakes you made the first time you wooed FAO Schwarz and Toys "Я" Us? The message may be the same, but it will be a lot more effective.

Sticky Fingers

When you like a piece of writing, ask yourself why. What's the author doing that works so well? Maybe it's something you can use in your own writing. But don't swipe another writer's words or style. The real you is always better than an imitation somebody else.

That doesn't mean we can't be influenced by writers we like. I've had crushes on more of them than I can remember, and I'm sure you've had your favorites, too. Our reading shapes our writing and our thinking, and it's supposed to. To love a piece of writing is to be influenced by it. Where did I get this brilliant insight? I stole it from Elizabeth Bishop.

In her *Collected Prose*, Bishop writes about her debt to the poet Marianne Moore: "I am sometimes appalled to think how much I may have unconsciously stolen from her. Perhaps we are all magpies."

30

Revise and Consent

GETTING TO THE
FINISH LINE

A former colleague of mine used to edit steamy romance novels and was ever on the alert for unintentional howlers: a sudden change in a lover's eye color, maybe, or an ancestral manse made of brick in one chapter and stone in the next. Then there was the pregnancy that didn't add up: the heroine was expecting for fifteen months. That was a nice catch.

Unfortunately, most of us don't have editors to save our butts. Our writing goes straight to our readers. If any butts are to be saved, we have to save them ourselves. That's why the wise revise.

Revising is more than fixing what's wrong; it's making

what's passable better. The Latin word *revisere* means "visit again." Revisiting your work isn't just an afterthought, something to do if you have the time. If you haven't revised, you're not finished.

There's no right or wrong way to revise. Some writers begin at the beginning and work their way through to the end. Others take care of obvious trouble spots first, then work their way through the whole piece. I'm in the second group. I make notes to myself as I write my first draft: "Insert formula for root beer"; "Check spelling of 'Bon Jovi' "; "Find cost of a dozen cantaloupes." In my first go-around, I take care of the notes, assuming I can find them. But it doesn't matter how you go about revising, as long as you do it.

The cruel reality of revision is that you sometimes have to dump what you love most. When the endorphins kick in and you've really got the subject by the throat, you're likely to repeat yourself. You'll write essentially the same sentence (or paragraph) three times in a row. Each one seems just right, a perfect gem, so you keep all three. I know it's tough, but when you revise, pick the version that says it best and drop the others. Your object is to move the point along, not to display your virtuosity.

Luckily, revising has never been so easy, thanks to the computer. The ability to search through a piece for particular words and phrases is something that Gibbon or Boswell might have killed for. A question that would otherwise be a major pain can now be answered in an instant: Have I mentioned Connie Francis yet? Where did I first refer to Uncle Eddie's stamp collection? How did I define *dithyramb*?

While I grumble about the imperfections of spell-checkers, mine does find those embarrassing word repetitions I can't see myself (*the the, with with, to to,* and so on). Thank you, computer.

The biggest benefit of revising on the computer, though, is the ease of moving around large blocks of type. Should this paragraph go there? Does that sentence sound better over here? If so, simply cut and paste. If you're not sure, you can copy and paste to see what the change would look like before committing yourself.

Naturally, there's a downside to technology. There are fewer scribbled-up manuscripts for future scholars to pore over. And since writing and revising are easier, many people write too much and then putter for too long, reluctant to let go.

Computer literate or not, good writers take pains to revise their work. Great writers take great pains. One of my favorites, William Trevor, types his short stories on paper, then uses the cut-and-paste method to move scenes around. "It's an untidy, rather dirty business, and it's messy," he once told an interviewer. "And the manuscript looks like a manuscript should look: It's absolutely filthy."

J. D. Salinger, on the other hand, is said to have used the facing pages of a ledger to do his revisions. He pasted a sheet of typewritten manuscript on one side, then wrote notes to himself on the other.

Balzac—a prolific note-taker, you'll recall—sweated bullets when he revised. He tirelessly rewrote, expanded, rearranged, cut, and corrected just to arrive at a first draft. When his publishers sent him the proofs, he rewrote, expanded, rearranged, cut, and corrected those.

When new proofs arrived he did the same thing. Printers loathed him.

Flaubert wrote *A Sentimental Education* twice and *The Temptation of St. Antony* three times, after intervals of many years. Jane Austen rewrote the ending of *Persuasion*. And Tiny Tim, the heart-wrenching tyke in *A Christmas Carol*, wasn't always Tiny Tim. Along the way, Dickens called him Small Sam, Little Larry, and Puny Pete. Even the "Bah!" in "Bah! Humbug!" was added later.

This doesn't mean you should fiddle with your writing just for the sake of fiddling. Don't fix what's not broken. The idea is to cast a critical eye on what you've written. If you're happy with it, congratulations. But if you're like the rest of us, you won't be happy with your first effort. What's more, you won't always know why you're not happy. And when you don't know what's wrong, you can't fix it. Here's a checklist of questions to ask as you revise.

The Final Analysis

Do I still like the beginning? Your ideas probably evolved as you wrote, so be sure the head now sits comfortably on the body. (Chapter 4)

Can I be simpler? Replace the long word with the short, the trendy with the tried-and-true, the pompous with the plain, the foreign with the domestic. (Chapter 6)

Can I be clearer? Every word, every sentence, every paragraph should be as clear as you can make it, with no chance that your reader might misunderstand. (Chapters 6, 9, 10)

Do I make sense? Check for any contradictions or lapses in logic. (Chapters 12, 17)

Do my numbers add up? Check every figure at least twice. (Chapter 19)

Do my sentences hang together? They should follow one another smoothly. Don't make them all the same length, or you'll put the reader to sleep. (Chapters 12, 13)

Do my verbs pull their weight? Replace the ninety-seven-pound weaklings and weed out unnecessary passives. And move verbs as close as you can to their subjects. (Chapters 7, 8, 21)

Do I need every modifier? Ditch any adjectives or adverbs you can do without. Be sure the ones you keep are where they belong—close to the nouns and verbs they describe. (Chapter 11)

Am I using the right image? Try to picture the imaginative flourishes in your writing. Careless images can create the wrong picture and make you look silly. (Chapters 11, 17)

Have I got rhythm? Listen to the sound of your writing. It should be rhythmic and easy to read, without unintentional jingles or rhymes. And the rhythm shouldn't clash with the subject matter. (Chapters 11, 24)

Am I playing in tune? Listen to the tone of your writing and make sure you like the person you hear. The tone should be in harmony with what you're writing about—not too flippant or too grim, for example—and it should be consistent. (Chapters 2, 20)

Can I trim? Cut whatever you can. If you've said something twice, make it once—even if you love both versions. (Chapters 6, 16, 21)

Have I made my case? Step back and consider what you've
   written. Did you say what you set out to say? Try to
   imagine the reader's overall impression. (Chapters 2, 3)
How's my grammar? Check your grammar, spelling, and
   punctuation. If you aren't sure, don't guess—look it up.
   (Chapter 18)

The Finish Line

The hardest part of revising is making yourself do it. The
second hardest is knowing when to stop. No piece of writing is ever perfect. There's always something that could be
better.

   Your favorite novel or history or memoir is just someone's last revision. Even *Hamlet* might have been im-
proved if Shakespeare had had another week to work on it.
I can hear his agent now: "Hey, Bill! These producers are
all over me like a cheap suit. Where's that last act?"

   At some point you have to stop futzing and say,
"That's it." But how do you know when you're done? Some
writers say an inner voice tells them when to stop, giving
them a "sense of completion." They're probably lying.

   Most of the writers I know don't stop because they are
suffused with satisfaction and feel some Zenlike fullness,
or emptiness, or whatever. They stop because they have to
stop someplace and this looks like a pretty good place. Either that or the piece is physically wrested from them. I've
seen this happen to reporters who won't let go.

   Like those reporters, I find that nothing beats a deadline. Ready or not, it's done when the bell goes off. But if
deadlines aren't a consideration, here's how to tell that
you're finished:

- You're hung up on trivialities. If you honestly can't decide between two piddling choices, it probably doesn't matter. Pick one.
- You're revising your revisions, and the revisions of the revisions.
- You're making things worse instead of better. (Don't forget to save the original.)
- It may not be perfect, but you gave it your best shot.
- It's good enough, and you're sick of looking at it.
- You like it. Even the person you ask for a second opinion likes it.

No doubt I've left things out. I had some fabulous notes on yellow stickies somewhere, but they must have come unstuck along the way. Let that be a lesson to you. No matter. There's always the revised edition.

Meanwhile, try to loosen up and have a good time. Writing can be a lot of fun. Nothing beats the feeling you get when you're writing something good—except the feeling you get when you're finished.

rtegdyrhrewyendjrmoclsjetwhfkldoflferhdtwy
tftjghrtgerfdtsyhejuogehtrysfertdgwrsteyhfushk
wgdhtjncgerebiduwerenhrsqeyifkdleystqnnaqmmxusd
epjstefb
ylryusfetrdgshuwyrtghsyeturheydf
yjfhrtegsfdytjhrjuktjfgersfegydthmburfdgsyegfhsuy

Appendix

Duck walks into a hardware store. "Got any duck food?" he quacks. "Sorry, no," says the proprietor. Duck leaves.

Next day the duck is back. "Got any duck food?" "No," says the proprietor. "I told you before. We don't carry it."

Next day he's back again: "Got any duck food?" The proprietor glares at him. "Look, buddy, we don't sell duck food. We never have and never will. And if you ask me that one more time, I'll nail your little webbed feet to the floor."

Next day the duck is back. "Got any nails?"

"We're out of nails today," says the proprietor.

"Got any duck food?"

Bibliography

The Careful Writer: A Modern Guide to English Usage. Theodore M. Bernstein. New York: Atheneum, 1977.

The Elements of Style. William Strunk, Jr., and E. B. White. 3d ed. New York: Macmillan, 1979.

A Mathematician Reads the Newspaper. John Allen Paulos. New York: Anchor Books, 1996.

The New York Public Library Writers' Guide to Style and Usage. Edited by Andrea J. Sutcliffe. New York: HarperCollins, 1994.

On Writing Well: An Informal Guide to Writing Nonfiction. William Zinsser. 5th ed. New York: HarperPerennial, 1994.

The Reader over Your Shoulder: A Handbook for Writers of English Prose. Robert Graves and Alan Hodge. New York: Macmillan, 1943.

Simple & Direct: A Rhetoric for Writers. Jacques Barzun. Revised ed. Chicago: University of Chicago Press, 1994.

Style: Toward Clarity and Grace. Joseph M. Williams. Chicago: University of Chicago Press, 1990.

Woe Is I: The Grammarphobe's Guide to Better English in Plain English. Patricia T. O'Conner. New York: Riverhead Books, 1998.

Writing with Style: Conversations on the Art of Writing. John R. Trimble. Englewood Cliffs, N.J.: Prentice-Hall, 1975.

Index